THE BALTIMORE CANON

THE BALTIMORE CANON

By
Thomas Archer

FIRST EDITION

Tier 7, Harvard, MA

Published by:

    TIER 7

    P.O. Box 920

    Harvard, MA 01451

All rights reserved. No portion of this book may be reproduced or transmitted in whole or in part by any means, electronic or mechanical, including photocopying, or by any information storage and retrieval system without written permission from the publisher.

Copyright © 2009 by Thomas Archer

First edition, first printing

Cover – Sunset from the lifeboat deck of the *BALTIMORE CANON*

Edited by Thomas S. R. Oldfield and Tamera S. C. Oldfield

ISBN 978-0-578-03388-4

Printed in the United States of America, and the United Kingdom

This book is dedicated to
those who are willing to take the required action
for the salvation of
those who are only willing to follow.

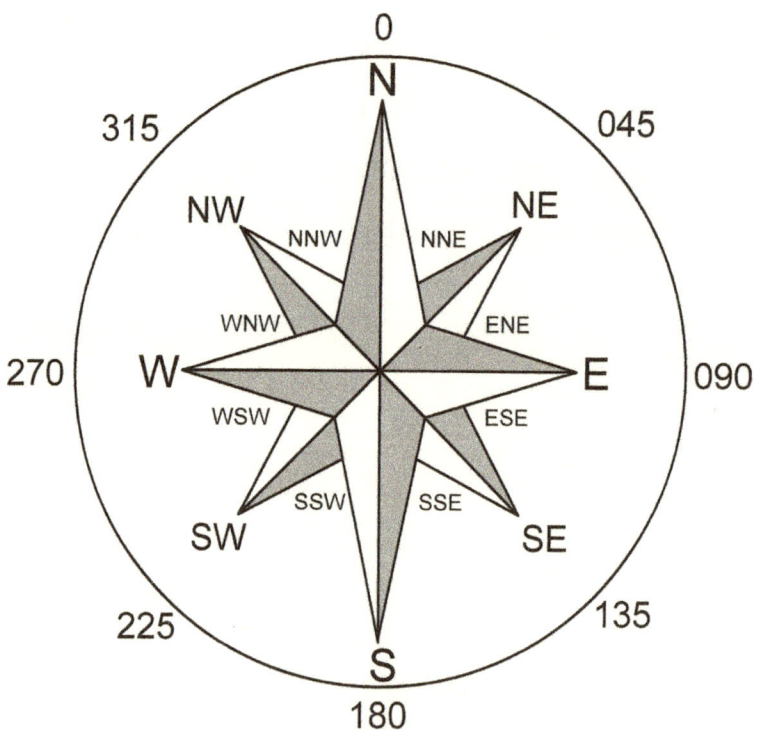

COMPASS ROSE

THE BALTIMORE CANON

The Waters of *THE BALTIMORE CANON*

Table of Contents

Introduction	11
Initiation	15
The First Day	22
To The Caribbean	31
South to Panama	39
The Panama Canal	46
Parita Bay	54
North to Yorktown	65
The Whistler	75
The Gulf of Mexico	84
Dilapidated	93
A New Friend	101
The Would Be Master	110
Perth Amboy	119
Baton Rouge	126
A New Crew	134
Back to Panama	142
Finally Ashore in Panama	151
More of the Same	160
Apprehension	165
Repairs	172

Contents continued

More Repairs	180
The Caretaker	186
Final Voyage	191
Epilogue	199
Addendum	202
Glossary	207

Illustrations

Compass Rose	6
The Waters of *THE BALTIMORE CANON*	8
Bridge Deck	24
Tank Top	49
Deck Valves	55
Deck Cargo Pipes	57
Tank Cargo Pipes	59
Docking Lines	155
Engine Order Telegraph	214

Photographs

Baltimore Canon Heading South	105
Oil Rigs in the Gulf of Mexico	105
Baltimore Canon Alongside the *British Renown*	145
Parita Bay	145

Introduction

The end of life as you know it, is not always a bad thing.

To survive aboard a ship, an officer has to live and breathe the ship. He has to know the sounds, good and bad, and the movement of the ship. He must develop a sense of the ship and surroundings, and they become part of him. His schedule is inflexible. The watches must be stood, the inspections made and the paperwork completed. The policies and procedures of ship's operations have been developed over the centuries at the cost of great human suffering and loss of life.

A ship's officer cannot be made in a matter of weeks or months. It takes years to develop the skills necessary, and learn from the sea itself the dangers and limitations of travel and transportation on the world's oceans. A ship's officer must be skilled in, not just have knowledge of; weather observation and reporting, terrestrial, celestial, and electronic navigation, mapping systems, fire fighting, maintenance and repair, labor management, small arms defense, international rules of the road, ocean currents, cargo handling, marlinspike seamanship, and a host of other things, all required for the safe operation and navigation of ships on the oceans.

Even as a new Third Officer, he will stand a watch on the bridge for eight hours a day at which times he will be in command of the ship, its operations and movements. His word will be law and will carry the threat of life and death. This is not a responsibility to be taken lightly or given to the callous individual who would put himself above the safety of the crew, but is reserved for those who have prepared for the responsibility and are willing to act in the interest and safety of all.

Command of the ship can only be in the hands of one person at a time and that person is usually the officer on watch. The presence of the captain on the bridge does not change the command, for that to happen the captain must say, "I'll take the con." The "con" means control. If the captain takes control, the watch officer makes an entry in the ship's log, noting the time. When the captain relinquishes control, he states, "You have the con." to the watch officer and another note is added to the ship's log. If the captain arrives on the bridge and starts issuing orders about the operation or navigation of the ship without taking the con, the watch officer will ask him "Captain are you taking the con?" The captain's answer will indicate who has the con. There can be no confusion on the point of who is in command of the ship.

A deck officer's duties include the navigation of the ship, and for him the sky is a celestial clock. He has azimuths to take, and sun lines and stars to use for navigation. He checks his compass on the sun at sunrise and sunset or Polaris, the North Star, during the night. He is in fact and action, an international citizen. He navigates with an intimate knowledge of the earth and heavens gained by centuries of exploration, and makes known to the world, newly discovered characteristics, without which men would perish at sea. He deals with merchants of all nations to develop a safe environment for travel and trade, enabling low risk, reliable international commerce.

This narrative takes place in the 1970s, a time before portable computers, satellite navigation systems, satellite phones, or even cell phones. It was a time when people waited for days, weeks, or sometimes months for news of loved ones at sea or abroad. Calls and wires were expensive, and most communication was through the mail, which although dependable in America, was on a fair effort basis in 3rd world countries like the island nations in the Caribbean, or the Latin American nations. Often, communications were sent by Morse code or short wave radio with prearranged times and frequencies, unless we were close enough to shore to use the VHF radio to connect through a marine operator.

On a coastwise ship, a seaman could be ashore every few days to make phone calls, or buy the things he needed. But if he was contracted to an ocean going ship, he could be at sea a month or two before stepping ashore. The typical sea term was between four and six months, and occasionally it would be four or six months before a sailor would step ashore. This was not a problem for a sailor with no relatives or shore ties, but led to great anxiety among the folks at home when wives and children waited for weeks or months for word of their loved ones.

The new officer, on the other hand, has his own problems. His new environment, good or bad, will cause great anxiety until he can assimilate with the ship and its crew. He will not be at ease until he becomes part of the ship. This can take weeks, but if it doesn't happen within the first month, it probably won't, and the officer had better look for another career. There are many academy graduates who sail less than a year before looking for work ashore.

A deck officer's life at sea is mostly solitary. The two men on the bridge deck with him are both busy about their work and should not be disturbed except as a matter of business. The lookout must do exactly that, without interruption. The helmsman keeps an eye on how the ship is steering and also cannot let his guard down; the bridge is not a place to hold coffee club meetings. The captain visits only at times of special circumstances, as in hostile waters or when making port; and interaction with the other officers only occurs in the first and last few minutes of the watch for the changeover.

Off watch, a deck officer rarely sees another deck officer; one is on the bridge, and the other is usually sleeping. There is some socializing during meals but even that is interrupted when one of the officers has to relieve the officer on the bridge for dinner.

This solitude is even more poignant for the new officer as he is both new to it, and it is exaggerated in his first few weeks while the other officers evaluate him and test his competency.

This is a true account of my experiences, as a new Third Officer, on my first ship, as recorded in my personal log. In relating these events in the form of a story, it might seem callous and maybe a bit harsh to dismiss a four hour watch or sometimes even an entire day aboard ship with just a line or two, but much of the time the work is just repetitive and mundane. The tales of sailors are of the extraordinary times, not of the ordinary. This is a story of both the ordinary and extraordinary, and includes the normally untold tedium, giving a glimpse of the real life experiences of a new ship's officer.

My personal log is not a diary. It is the actual account, in its truest form of what happened on my watch, and during the exercise of my duties. It is curt and factual, and contains information not always available in the ship's log. It is a compilation of timed statements with entries such as "1720 2/0 returned", which means that at 1720 or 5:20 pm, the second officer returned to the bridge after having gone below to the mess deck for dinner while the third mate stood by for him on the bridge. It also implies that the second mate was standing the 4-8 watch and was on the bridge from 0400-0800 (4am-8am) and 1600-2000 (4pm-8pm), requiring someone (usually the third mate), to stand in for him as the ship cannot be underway without an officer on the bridge.

This book is written in the first person, in prose to make easier reading, and the names of some of the ships and crew members have been changed to protect the innocent.

Archer, 2009

Chapter 1

INITIATION

I suppose every sailor best remembers his first voyage on his first ship. It's the beginning of a metamorphosis; a life changing experience from the comfort and safety of the small known world, to the unchained natural forces of wind driven seas on the boundless oceans.

I won't mislead you; I didn't accidentally or unexpectedly find myself shipped out to sea the day after a long night of carousing bars and passing out in an alley; I wasn't shanghaied. I had prepared for this journey; I knew what I was getting into, or so I thought. I had attended the academy for four years, studying with the tenacity of one who is paying for his-own education. I learned all of the things that I was supposed to, practiced the skills required until I was proficient, and disciplined myself, preparing for the rigors of seaboard life. But this is not how it began.

Although I don't like to admit it, I know exactly how I ended up as a merchant mariner. It started in high school with the "dream". Not the dream about fitting into society, or getting a good job, or even being rich and famous, although the rich part was high on the list. The dream was to have money, and a lot of free time – without ending up behind a desk. As I found out a little later, we don't always get what we ask for.

Someone pointed me to the academy, with some advice about something that I don't remember, and the phrases "they have a ship" and "training outside the classroom". There were a lot of other things in there but they didn't seem important at the time. When I got to the academy, I found out how important those other things were, for example; military, uniforms, discipline, and others I won't bore you with. It seems there was a lot of work involved in staying out from behind a desk, including quite a bit that required being behind a desk.

The first year I didn't understand what I was doing or what I was getting into; and with the workload, I didn't spend much time thinking about it. We had all of the classes necessary to earn our four-year academic degrees interlaced with the additional courses required to obtain a merchant marine officer's license. I thought the training ship was permanently attached to the dock – it didn't occur to me that it was actually floating and could move. After all, it was huge – over 500 feet long, and nothing seemed to work on it. That image was modified somewhat when I found out that we had to spend our summer vacation at sea aboard it. And I didn't know that I was studying to be a ship's officer, or even what a ship's officer did.

Over the next two years, I learned quite a bit about the merchant marine, but I never really thought that I would ship out. It wasn't until late in my last year, after I had passed the license examinations that I decided to try to get a position on a ship.

After graduating that summer, I went down to the union hall (that seemed to be the thing to do) to inquire about a position. When I presented my license, the dispatcher asked if I was ready to go. I replied that I was but that I would like some advance notice so I could pack. I was told to go home, settle my affairs, pack my sack, and then call in when I was ready to go. Settle my affairs? That didn't sound good.

Two weeks later I called in to get on the list. The delay was my procrastination. Actually, I was packed the next day and I had no affairs to settle – rather sad when you think about it. I just wasn't sure that I wanted to be somewhere that I had to settle my affairs to get to. The dispatcher told me that from that moment on, my job was to stand by the phone, Monday through Friday, from eight in the morning until five in the evening. If I didn't answer the phone, they would move on to the next name on the list, and my name would go to the bottom. I could expect a call at any time, but it would probably be a week out.

I waited. Two weeks later the phone rang. "Hello."

"Is this Tom?"

"Yes." I replied.

"Are your bags packed?"

"Yes." I replied again.

"The *BALTIMORE CANON* will be in Newport News, Virginia. She's a supertanker, come in from the Bahamas, heading out to the Mediterranean. Do you want her?"

"Yes I do." I answered.

"There will be a ticket waiting for you at the Delta counter at La Guardia Airport on Wednesday for an 11:00 morning flight. When you get off the plane down there, your driver will be holding a sign up with your name on it. Go with him, he knows where to go. Got it?"

"Yes. How long will I be gone?"

"Can you do six months?"

"Yes"

"Great, good luck." He hung up.

So, that was it. It was all set, and I had two days to chicken out. I had never traveled alone before so I had some reservations about this pending ordeal.

I followed the instructions; and got a limo to the airport, and my plane ticket was waiting for me at the counter. I got on the right plane and arrived at the correct destination, with the correct baggage. The taxi driver even seemed to know where the place was that I wanted to get to. So...if I had done it correctly, why was I sitting by myself on the edge of a dock marked "ENTER AT YOUR OWN RISK"? The dock was very long, and in really bad shape, and no one else was there.

While I waited there, for several hours, my thoughts were not comforting. Was I at the right place? Was I there at the right time or even on the right day? What would I do if the ship was delayed – for days? The sun had set. What if the ship had already come and gone? It was getting dark. Apprehension is worse in the dark.

Off in the distance I heard the motor of a small boat. I could barely make out the silhouette as it approached. A short time later the bow of the skiff nosed up onto the mud bank as the pilot cut off the motor and tipped it forward.

"Are you the new third?" It was an old raspy voice.

"Yes sir."

"Well get your gear in."

I loaded my gear, which sat the skiff hard on the mud, then lifted the bow off the mud and pushed out, hopping aboard as the pilot started the motor. We were very low in the water indeed but managed the distance without swamping though we shipped a few wavelets over the side. He coasted up to an old rope ladder and cut the motor.

"Grab that." He said pointing to the ladder.

I took hold of the ladder while holding onto the thwart to keep us alongside. As I looked up at my new home, I was amazed at how old and rusty the ship was. Was this what our merchant marine was made up of, a fleet of rusting hulks, not far from the scrap yards and razor blades? At that point my greatest hope was that it wouldn't sink while I was on it. A rope dropped into the boat from above and my baggage was sent up to the deck hands one piece at a time. As the last one went up, the old pilot started the motor and I grabbed both sides of the ladder while stepping on the first rung. The rope stretched under my weight as the skiff moved away and I was only about a foot off the water with thirty feet to go up. I quickly placed my other foot on the next rung, remembering my schooling – always have three points of contact in the event that one fails. That ladder was in bad shape and any part could fail. I climbed slowly and carefully testing each rung before I put my weight on it.

"Welcome aboard mate." I heard as I gained the deck.

"Thanks" I replied. "Which way to the captain's office?"

"Up that ladder, then up three more."

From the deck, the view was worse, rusting steel bleeding through yellowed white paint; at least it was less visible through the red deck paint. The smell of oily rusted steel permeated the air. Even today, when I come across this smell, the vision of this first view besets me along with an anxiety that lurks about for an hour or so.

I made my way to the captain's office to sign the ship's articles. After presenting my license, and signing, I was curtly told to stow my gear in the ship's hospital, post my license in the frame by the bridge door, and get some rest because I would be on the 12-4 watch. I thought that was unusual because I had learned in school that the third mate gets the 8-12 watch so the captain can keep an eye on him. The third mate is the least experienced and therefore requires the closest supervision. It is not prudent to leave a green third officer in command of any ship, especially an oil tanker; and I was as green as they came.

I was called by the watch around midnight, to test the ship's equipment for departure. The purpose of this is to turn on all of the ship's bridge equipment and verify that it is working before attempting to get the ship underway, such as; the steering units, the radar units, the running lights, engine order telegraph, compasses – gyro and magnetic, fire and smoke indicator systems, etc. This was not easy, being unfamiliar with the ship and with the job, but I accomplished the task with the help of my notebook from school and then familiarized myself with the bridge and chart room. The proper charts being in order, and the equipment functioning properly, I posted the helm and awaited the arrival of the captain and pilot on the bridge.

The bridge, so dark, lonely, and dormant, immediately came alive with the arrival of the captain. The radios squawked, tugs came along side, the pilot arrived, deck crews fore and aft, lines let go, and amidst the noise I relayed the engine orders to the engineer and made the entries in the Bell Book. The Bell Book is a small book placed next to the Engine Order Telegraph when maneuvering, for logging all engine orders by symbol, with the time they are given.

I was surprised at what was expected of me within just a few hours of joining the ship, especially when the captain knew that I had never sailed before. But the real surprise came when the ship cleared the entrance to Chesapeake Bay. The pilot had departed inside the breakwaters of Chesapeake Bay and the captain, who I expected would not let me out of his sight on my first watch, very bluntly told me to keep her on the track, and that he would see me in the morning. Then, without delay, he left the bridge.

Suddenly it was terribly dark and quiet on the bridge. There are no lights on the bridge of a ship at night. All lights are put out to ensure the mate can see small, lighted objects in the water. The only noise is the drone of the ship's engine and the traffic coming over the ship's VHF radio. Even the illumination from the ship's electronic equipment is dimmed so low that it is barely visible to the eyes of the mate's night vision. Sometimes it is rather eerie on a ship's bridge at night. I hadn't experienced this before, and didn't notice with all the activity. Now, alone with the helmsman, it seemed so much darker and quieter.

Although I'd had the education and training necessary, I had very little experience and barely any confidence at all. I was a little overwhelmed by the circumstances, as I looked out across the Gulf Stream at hundreds of ships and small craft knowing that I had to navigate a 600 foot tanker amidst them. But it wasn't until the ship was about a half mile off course that I felt the gravity of the situation. Until that time I had felt like an observer. I had suddenly become the one who had to do something – take action. We were steering a course of 161 and drifting east. Would this helmsman, who was in his sixties and had been sailing for forty years, do what I (who had been sailing for less than an hour) told him to do? Would I tell him to do the right thing? Would I use the correct language? What would he do? Would he say no? Would he ask a question that I didn't know the answer to? Would he laugh?

"Five degrees right rudder" said a voice that I didn't recognize.

"Five degrees right rudder" the helmsman repeated.

"Steady on 165" I commanded.

"Steady on 165" He repeated.

"She's steady on 165" he added a few minutes later.

I had given my first commands on my first watch on my first ship. And they were the correct words at the proper time and caused the required action. Nothing heroic, not even urgent or unusual, but delivered with the calm, even, commanding posture of a ship's officer – which I now was.

Chapter 2

The First Day

When studying navigation at the academy we used charts for the East Coast of North America; probably because we were located in that region. Navigation exams were difficult because the passing grade was 90%; and that was considered lenient because no one wanted a 90% navigator on the bridge of a ship. One error in judgment by the navigator of a supertanker could wipe out the environmental habitat from Key West to Cape Hatteras (an eight hundred mile stretch on the south east coast of the United States); or as we saw in 1989, the environment of Prince William Sound in Alaska.

But, as great as the pressure of passing the exam was, it was small compared to the practical application of those principles, on site as the responsible officer, navigating the coastal waters of the western Atlantic Ocean and Caribbean Sea, two of the most remarkable and treacherous regions of the world. As evidenced by the number of wrecks and disappearances, the vast regions of shallows amidst deep canyons, and swift ocean currents, combined with the sharp water temperature gradients, create congested traffic patterns with less than ideal weather conditions.

My first voyage as a ship's officer was to be from Newport News in Chesapeake Bay to Bahia Parita in Panama, to take on a load of crude oil, and discharge it to a port on the east or Gulf Coast. That being said, my first ship was a sort of oil tanker. I say sort of because it started out in the 40's as a small T-2 tanker and was jumboized in the 60's. Basically they cut out the middle of the ship and added a much larger section giving a greater carrying capacity with an underpowered plant and questionable steering characteristics. By the time I joined, it was a big rusting hulk whose age was catching up to it. What it was not was a supertanker coming from the Bahamas on its way to the Mediterranean as the union dispatcher had indicated.

The *BALTIMORE CANON* was six hundred feet long and eighty-five feet wide. It had a forecastle at the bow, which is an enclosed area used for storage, raising the deck at the bow section above the main deck by about ten feet. The main house, including the bridge, living quarters, mess halls, and engine space, was all the way aft.

The bridge house was only about twenty feet square, the front half outfitted as the wheel house or bridge, and the back half cut up into a number of rooms; the chart room for navigation and plotting, the gyro room housing a four foot tall gyroscopic compass, the sea cabin for the captain to rest without leaving the bridge, and a pantry for refreshment while on watch.

The wheelhouse was crammed with equipment, all necessary and required by law. There were two radar units, usually only one working; two steering consoles, one electric and one hydraulic; a wooden compass binnacle and stand showing six colors of paint; a VHF radio for inter-ship and ship to shore communications; a smoke pipe detecting system; the navigation light system; a sound powered phone for intra-ship communications; voice tubes to the captain's room, radio room and flying bridge (this is the open air deck directly above the wheelhouse with its own compass and steering); the engine order telegraph; international code signal flag set; and various indicators and recorders mounted on the bulkheads. Visibility was provided by three portholes forward and one on each side requiring me to spend most of my watch time on the bridge wing (there is a wing on each side of the bridge, extending the working area of the officer out to the sides of the ship when the wheelhouse is so small that it doesn't

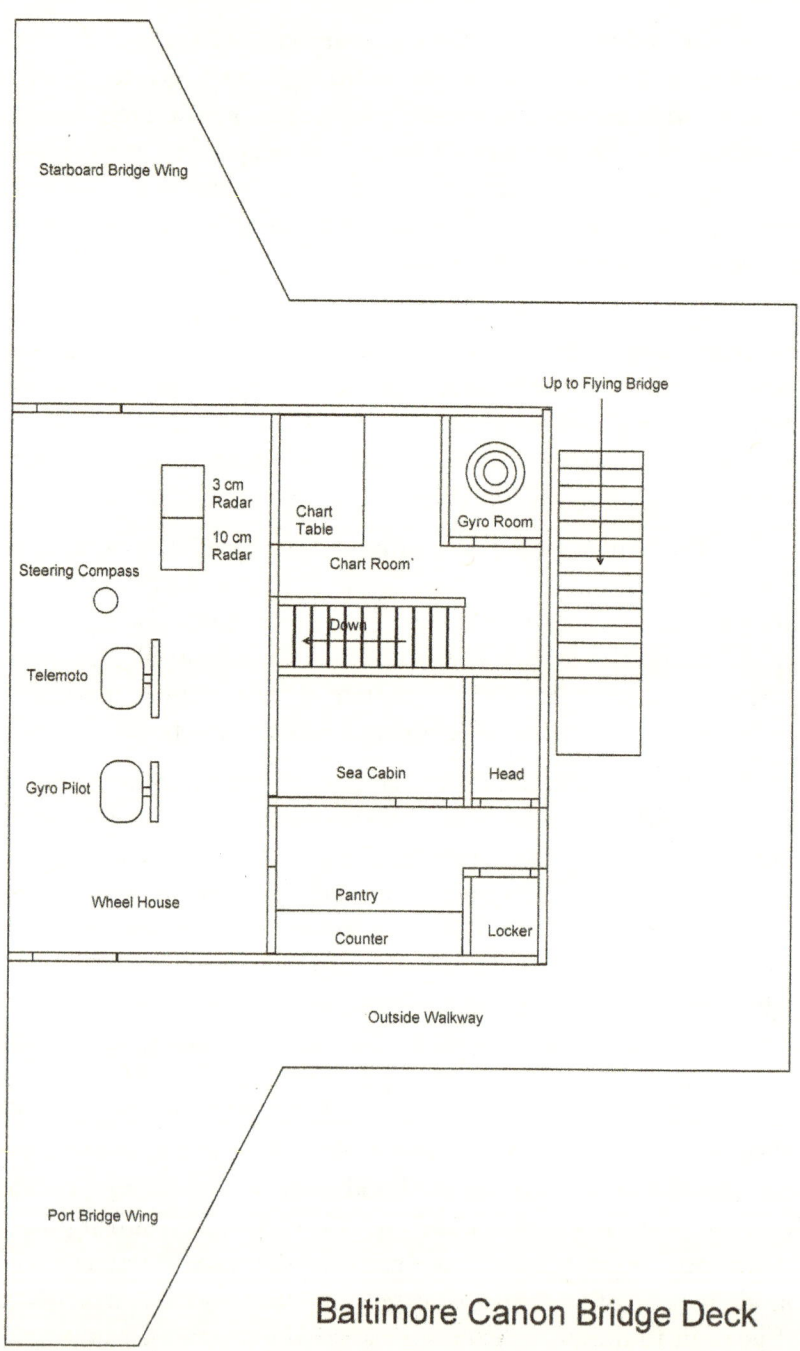

Baltimore Canon Bridge Deck

reach out to the sides of the ship). Paint was peeling from the overhead and bulkheads and the floor surface was cracked and worn through in several places. Maintenance had a low priority on this tub, and cosmetics had none.

We took departure from the Chesapeake Bay sea buoy on my watch and proceeded SSE, traveling along the coast towards Cape Hatteras. The water was shallow in this area and the traffic was heavy. The ship was in light ballast, meaning with no cargo and just enough extra seawater loaded to keep the prop and rudder in the water. In this condition, the ship vibrated heavily and had a mean roll in light seas. It was hard to line up a sight (take a bearing on a fixed point on land) in that condition because the gyro repeaters are on the bridge wings where the roll is exaggerated. We had a twelve foot drag, meaning the bow was higher than the stern by twelve feet; this was the normal ballasted condition of a tanker. In that condition, there was a section of water in front of the ship about eight miles out that was not visible from the bridge. On some ships in ballast, the bow completely obstructs the view to the horizon.

The watch went quietly and quickly as I constantly fixed the ship's position on the chart, making sure we were where we should be. A grounding can really ruin your day, especially if it's your first day. The second mate took the watch at 0348, twelve minutes before eight bells. This is standard procedure in the merchant marine; the watch is relieved twelve minutes before the hour so the outgoing officer has some time to fill in his replacement on traffic, location and weather, and fill in the logbook, remaining on the bridge for a few minutes in case there are any questions.

After filling out the ship's log and my own personal log I went below to get settled. First I stopped in sickbay, picked up my sack, and dropped it off in my room, two levels below the bridge, then went down to the mess hall on the main deck, two levels below my room to see if there was anything to eat at four in the morning. There was – lots. The kitchen was closed but the cook left out enough food for the night. With round the clock shifts, food was always made available. After my early morning snack I started back to my room to unpack.

Ships are kept dark at night, with no lights showing outside, except the navigational lights. The navigational lights are used to indicate to others the approximate size, heading, and characteristics of the vessel. One additional light showing could be enough to confuse another ship's officer, leading him to take action that he shouldn't and cause a collision.

The mess hall was on the main deck, and there was no inside access between the officers deck and the main deck. I had left the bridge with most of my night vision intact, so getting to the mess hall was easy. After being in the brightly lit mess hall for a half hour I had no night vision left. To get back, I had to go forward through a watertight door to the open weather deck and up a ladder to another weather deck to get access to the officer's deck.

There are two main types of doors on a ship, watertight doors, and standard doors. Watertight doors are rectangular with rounded corners, made of heavy steel and have a levers, or dogs, at all four corners, or a wheel action that secures all four corners. These are located at all main deck entrances and all passages through watertight bulkheads. You generally have to step up at least a foot to get through these, and all exterior doors are closed at night to darken the ship. The standard interior doors are steel and look normal except the threshold is about four inches high to stop the flow of water, should any get through the watertight doors when in use during heavy seas – this takes getting used to. As I said, getting to the mess deck was easy; as I opened the doors, I had enough light to see the next ladder; going back was different. As I pushed open the watertight door to the main deck, against the wind, the damp salty breeze hit me in the face. I stepped through and went to shut it, but the wind took care of that for me, closing off all light. All was black.

I stood on the main deck in the dark for a few minutes waiting for my night vision, thinking that it would start to get light in another hour or so anyway. Most ships travel at between 12 and 25 knots (about 15 to 30 mph) so there is always wind and the noise it makes, traveling through the ship. The ship was still rolling and I could hear the bow hitting the sea and the sea coming down the side of the ship. After a few minutes I could see the shore lights moving with the horizon. A few minutes later I could see the ladder in the starlight and grabbed the railing to climb up to the next deck. The railing was damp and had a dirty feel to it; a combination of chipped paint, rust and light coat of brine. The next deck was a raised weather deck, which means that it was also open to the weather. Deck and mechanical equipment and lines were stored here for easy access while maintaining some protection from the seas that would wash over the main deck in storms. I was looking for a ladder located amidships about fifty feet back from the forward bulkhead. It was darker in this area because it was covered, save for a crack of light seeping through the bottom of the door at the top of the ladder. It was a strange type of ladder; there was no platform at the top, outside the door, so you had to hang on with one hand while you opened the door with the other. As I approached the ladder I could hear sounds that indicated conversation on the other side of the door. I listened for a few minutes but couldn't make out any words. As I climbed the ladder and approached the door, the noise increased in volume. The sounds were halfway between words and the wind; and I could hear them whistling under the door. As I opened the door, harsh light flooded the space, temporarily blinding me again. No one was in the small hallway on the other side of the door; so it must have been the wind. Each morning for the next six months, I would approach this door in the dark and just for a moment stop and listen. And each time, I could almost make out the words.

  I entered my small room; just enough room for a rack, dresser, and desk. I stowed my gear and rested on the rack. My watch indicated 0448. I shut my eyes and took in the roll of the ship. There was a slight pitch now also. The steam engine droned on, the ballasted ship shuddered.

  Somewhere in the distance there was a knock on a door – "1115 mate, warm and sunny". I raised my arm and checked my watch -1115. I had just lain down. I sat up, and reached over to open the cover on the porthole. Sun light flooded in. I grabbed the rail and swung my legs over the side of the bunk; I hadn't even taken my shoes off. The bathroom that was located at the end of the cabin would press a contortionist to utilize. The sink was big enough for my hands but not my face; the shower could only be accessed sideways, and the toilet – well the operative word here would be balance. I cleaned up and went down to the mess hall. The tables were set with cloths and dishes, and the waiter indicated the seat reserved for me and pointed to the menu. After my selections were placed before me, I was quizzed on whether I liked coffee and preferred it before, during, or after the meal; if I would be having breakfast (the mate on the ghost watch rarely takes breakfast); and various other preferences. I learned to send word to the mess hall when my schedule changed for any reason; because if I didn't show up, the mess man would have someone track me down. I also got the idea that I might find no setting for me at the table if I showed up unexpectedly. Many times over the years meals were served to me on the bridge when I was unable to leave. It didn't take long for my waiter to learn my taste so I would simply point to something on the menu and watch. A nod meant I would like it and a shake of the head meant it was not to my taste. He also seemed to know if I wanted dessert or not. He wasn't my personal waiter, but it seemed like he was.

At 1148 I was on the bridge relieving the other third mate. He left no clear position, only a guess, and disappeared rather quickly. I fixed the ship's position by LORAN A, something not known on ship's today, as about fifty miles off Cape Hatteras, crossing the main current of the Gulf Stream heading SSE.

LORAN is an acronym standing for LOng RAnge Navigation or LOng Range Aid to Navigation depending on whom you ask. It is an electronic time pulse system with land based transmitters along coastal areas, and shipboard receivers measuring time delay between pulses. Coastal charts had LORAN signal line overlays for position plotting. The LORAN A system, developed during the second world war, was accurate enough to provide navigational capability up to a thousand miles off the coast and was still in use in the seventies and early 1980 but it was tedious to use. Each station had to be tuned in and the signals were synchronized in three successive stages each time you wanted to establish a position. That was a time consuming process and though good for the time, tedious and inaccurate compared to the LORAN C system replacing it. LORAN C maintained two stations tuned in and gave a continuous digital readout of the time delay. The *BALTIMORE CANON* had both of these systems but seemed to use LORAN A almost exclusively. The old third mate didn't seem to like either of them and usually turned them off while he was on watch.

The Gulf Stream is one of the most unusual ocean currents in the world. It takes water from the North Atlantic Equatorial Current flowing through the Caribbean coming into the Gulf of Mexico between Cuba and Honduras, and from the same, coming through the Bahamas, and sends it north along the east coast at speeds up to four knots. Cape Hatteras, a point of land that juts out from the mainland, pushes the Gulf Stream north-east, where it starts to dissipate, running up against the Labrador Current. The two currents don't mix though, instead, they create a cold wall, and you can see the difference in color (indigo/aqua) between the two. While running between twenty and one hundred miles off the coast, the Gulf Stream also sends a counter current south, closer to shore.

We were heading SSE, crossing the Gulf Stream to travel south outside of the current. The watch was uneventful; I changed over to the next chart, sighted only one ship, and all navigation was by LORAN A. I set up my sextant, synchronized my watch with the chronometer, and checked the publications to see that they were all up to date in preparation for the next day's navigation challenges. At about 1400 I was questioned about the noon report, something I knew nothing about. Every day at sea, the 12-4 officer makes out the noon report and sends copies to the captain, chief engineer, radio operator and crew's mess. The ship's performance is calculated from noon to noon, or on the first day from departure to noon, on the last day from noon to arrival. I found the pad and set to work filling in the information; latitude, longitude, course made good, speed made good, wind and sea conditions, distance, length of day (the first and last days would normally be less then 24 hours), stoppages, and distance to go. It was a few hours late that day.

We were still in the current when the second mate relieved the watch, and would be for at least another three hours. I went below and discovered that my room had been cleaned and there were two new bars of soap on my desk. I put one in the bathroom and the other in the top drawer of the desk. There were some forms in the top drawer that looked important; a Port Log, and a Safety Log. I planed to ask the second mate about them when I relieved him for dinner. On opening the bottom drawer, I found it packed full of soap. I was later to find that the contract called for each sailor to receive two bars of good quality soap per week, and use them or not, two more would arrive every week. I tried to wedge my additional new bar into the bottom drawer but it wouldn't fit so I put it back in the top drawer. I was on that ship for 27 weeks and I got my full measure — 54 bars of soap.

Chapter 3

To the Caribbean

I relieved the second mate at 1655 for dinner. We were about one hundred and thirty miles off the coast still heading SSE, on the outer fringes of the Gulf Stream. There was no traffic so I took a sun line and it worked out well. A sun line is a line of position using the sun as a reference point by bearing and altitude as compared to a land bearing on a coastal point. I wanted to test my accuracy while I still had an electronic means to fix the position. LORAN A accuracy would diminish as we departed the US coastal area.

On his return at 1715, the second mate explained the noon report as well as the port log and safety log to me. I would have to start filling out the port log for Yorktown that night so it could be mailed back to the home office when we reached Panama. I went below for dinner. The dining room was about half full, each officer with his own place. It would never be more than half full because a third of the crew was always on watch, and others would be sleeping or working on maintenance. No one spoke to me; it was a quiet dinner.

Later on I reviewed the port log paperwork and the previously completed forms. I would need some info from the ship's log and some from the chief mate before I started the calculations. The chief mate didn't stand a watch on this ship, and I had only seen him in passing a few times. I would have to catch him in the morning on deck. I slept from 1930 until my call at

2330, and took the watch at 2348. The other third mate left no certain position so I had to work that out before I did anything else.

The crew on the *BALTIMORE CANON* numbered forty-three with five deck officers and five engineering officers. The captain and chief engineer were on call at all times; the chief mate and first engineer were both day workers; and the other officers each stood two, four hour watches each day and had other daytime duties as well. I was the youngest officer by at least eight years; the second mate was in his thirties, the chief mate in his sixties, the other third mate past seventy, and the captain, eighty-something. The average age of a merchant mariner at that time was about fifty five and the crew of the *BALTIMORE CANON* fit right in. On my watch I had two able body seamen and one ordinary seaman, none under fifty. One was always at the helm steering or monitoring the autopilot (yes, it worked, mostly, but not always). Another was always on lookout, and the third was on break in the crew's mess hall standing by the phone.

An ordinary seaman was the least experienced member of the deck department and was really just an apprentice. They weren't allowed to handle a steering shift until they could demonstrate to the officer of the watch that they were capable. This was accomplished under the supervision of an able body seaman and verified by the course recorder. The able body seaman was experienced, lifeboat certified, and capable of steering the ship and handling the deck machinery used in handling lines and working the anchor.

I was warned by the second mate that we had to keep an eye on the captain because he was "starting to loose it". I agreed; he cut me loose at the entrance of Chesapeake Bay. I should have warned the second mate that he also needed to keep an eye on me, he had his hands full, a captain with memory problems; a third mate who never seemed to know where he was; and me.

There was a section of water in the Atlantic that we were transiting at that moment with a green third mate at the con, called the Bermuda Triangle. This triangle is bounded by Cape Hatteras, the island of Bermuda (five hundred and forty miles southeast of Cape Hatteras, and the Northeast Providence Channel, south of the Great Abaco Island in the Bahamas or more specifically, a small section of water in that channel called the Hole In The Wall.

This section of water is notorious for ships grounding, sinking and disappearing, and a half hour study of a chart of the waters would make the reason obvious even to the novice. The Bahamas is a group of islands that rise out of Atlantic about forty-five miles off the southeast coast of Florida. The group is about two hundred miles wide and five hundred miles long, and most of the water in that area is less than 20 feet deep with a good portion less than 3 feet deep. The water around this group of islands is very deep (thousands of feet deep) and rises quickly to this plateau. There are several wide, deep passages through these islands but you have to know where they are. Ships crossing the North Atlantic and making for the Gulf of Mexico have few choices. They will either fight the Gulf Stream, not very economical; cross the Stream and hug the coast of Florida, a traffic nightmare; go through the Hole In The Wall picking up speed in the Providence Channels and then bucking the current in the Straits of Florida, not great but better; or go around Cuba and come in from the south, the long way around. There is a channel between Cuba and the Great Bahama Bank called the Old Bahama Channel but its only ten miles wide at parts and Cuba is very possessive about its twelve mile territorial limit – they will come and get you, and haul you into port where you will wait while the international incident is resolved, national apologies are made and officials are paid off. This will cost far more than the two days you attempted to shave off your voyage.

We were heading for the eastern Bahamas, still two and a half days away, and I had just altered our heading to due south. We would pass the Hole In The Wall in a day and a half, well to the east of it, and would expect crossing traffic in that area. It was a clear night with scattered clouds and a moderate sea. The moon was still up and it was bright enough to see the horizon beneath it. The buzzer sounded on the navigational light panel, and the light indicated that the stern light had gone out. I flipped the switch but the backup light failed also. I asked AB Parle if there was a light to rig on the stern and he replied that there was. It sounded like this was not an unusual event. I told him to go aft and rig the light when the ordinary relieved him. "Sure thing Mate" was his only response. Ordinary Seaman Galvan arrived at 0228 to take the helm.

"She's headed One Eight Zero on the gyro pilot, pulling to the right." Parle announced.

"One Eight Zero on the gyro" Galvan replied.

"Going to rig the light Mate" Parle stated as he left the bridge.

At 0340 the sound powered phone rang.

"Bridge" I answered. There was a muffled voice on the receiver.

"Hey Mate, I rigged that stern light; it's all set."

"Thanks" I answered and hung up.

The sound-powered phone was powered by crystals. There was no electricity or other power source involved except the electric charge generated by the side crank to ring the bell at the other end, so the phone still worked when the ship lost power.

To make a call you would set the station dial on the front to make contact for the station you wanted to ring; then you would crank the side lever to send a charge to the destination station ringer, and listen for someone to answer. It sounded like they were talking with their hands covering their mouth. To talk, you had to cup your hand over the mouthpiece and speak loudly. These phones worked fairly well except when trying to talk to an engineer at the station located between the boilers where the normal sound level is about 120 decibels.

In water over 2600 fathoms or 15000 feet deep, we were averaging about fifteen knots, and we were still tracking on LORAN A. I had to maneuver for a crossing ship, probably headed for northern Europe. The second mate arrived on time and I filled him in on the traffic, heading, and stern light situation. Then I went back to the chart room and filled out the log. There was a red filter on the chart table light allowing us to leave the door to the bridge open at night. It was by that red light that I filled out the log, and it was by that red light that I couldn't see certain red lines on the pages of the logbook that made me out to be rather sloppy in the normal daylight by which the Captain reviewed the log.

I went below for a snack and returned to my room, pausing momentarily on the ladder outside the hallway door in the tween deck space to see if I could make out any words whistling under that door, but I couldn't – although I thought, for a moment...

I was up early that morning hunting down the chief mate to get some assistance with the Port Log. Lunch was quiet, the only other officer in the mess was one of the third engineers.

Again, on the bridge, the old third mate had no position on the chart, and yelled out the course on his way out. We were still heading south, toward Crooked Island. I took the local apparent noon or LAN sight and fixed the ships position on the chart, then filled out and distributed the noon report. LAN is when the sun is bearing due south or north as it crosses the exact longitude or meridian the ship is located on. The line of position that comes from taking the altitude, by sextant, of the sun at its maximum height gives the exact latitude the ship is on. There is more detail involved, but the basics are sufficient for now.

There was a new form on the chart table – the weather report form. This report form was about 16 inches long and 30 inches wide. The officers on American ocean going ships have to fill out this report every 6 hours based on Greenwich Mean Time when the ship is at sea. If you've ever wondered how they know the weather across the oceans, this report is your answer. There were about 30 items that had to be filled out; wet and dry bulb temperatures, direction and length of sea swells, direction and height of wind waves and which of 27 cloud types were present. A ship's officer has to be a certified weather observer and be able to create the weather maps you see on the news today, from tabulated data. I spent about an hour filling that report out before sending it to the radio room. With practice I got a lot faster at it; and that was good because the time between reports is reduced in areas of heavy weather. The data we wired in was compiled by NOAA (National Oceanographic and Atmospheric Administration), and weather maps were generated and sent to all ships by facsimile every 6 hours. Legibility varied by the distance offshore and weather conditions local to the ship. That meant, in poorest weather conditions crossing an ocean, when we needed the reports the most, they were almost undecipherable.

I measured the distance to Crooked Island; we would pass it on my watch at about 1400 or about two in the afternoon. I only saw two ships on this watch, both going our way; I expected more as we approached the Bahamas. The Second Mate was on time and I went below for an hour to work on the port log. When I returned to the bridge at 1655, there was a third ship on the port side, broad on the beam, heading SW toward the Hole; it would cross behind us. We were still three hundred miles from Crooked Island.

At 1720 I went below for dinner. It was another quiet dinner; I neither spoke, nor was spoken to. After dinner I worked on the Port Log until 2030 and retired for a few hours before watch.

The ghost watch was uneventful. We were south of the traffic area and too far out for any smaller craft. Its unusual for a third mate to be taking night sights, but I liked celestial navigation and found that I had an aptitude for it while I was at the academy. I took an azimuth off Polaris, the official name for the North Star, which showed gyro error at .6 E, well within standards. The moon was still up and provided a sufficient horizon, so I took out my stopwatch and sextant, and was able to get a night sight on Alkaid, one of the navigable stars in Ursa Major also known as the Big Dipper. In celestial navigation, time is as critical as altitude; the earth turns one nautical mile at the equator every 4 seconds so I liked half second accuracy for my work. The sight worked out well but it took me half an hour to do it. I would have to improve on that in the next few months.

I was up for breakfast that morning to my waiter's surprise, and turned in the port log to the chief mate. He told me to see him in a day or so, after I did my safety inspection, to start going over the cargo system.

As the Safety Officer, I had to perform a complete safety inspection once a week, and an additional fire extinguisher check the day before arriving in port. The engineers seemed to have a lot of small fires in the engine room requiring the extinguishers to be recharged every time we hit port. They also seemed to neglect to tell any one that they had used them so I had to go around weighing them. That may not sound bad, but there were twenty-six of them scattered over five decks in the engine space. In all, there were seven fire axes that had to be in place, twenty one fire stations with hoses and nozzles that had to be in good working condition, forty-two CO_2 fire extinguishers to be weighed and replaced with spares when used, one mechanical foam room, one emergency diesel room, three foam monitor stations, two lifeboats, an EPIRB (emergency position indicating radio beacon), two automatic watertight doors, and sixteen life rings with beacons. It took me three days to find all that stuff the first time.

At 1148 I was at the con, steering 200 and entering the Crooked Island Passage with nothing in sight yet. I took care of the noon business and turned on the radar. The captain didn't like using the radar units as they were old, and the magnetrons had a limited life, one was already dead; but I wanted a range off Crooked Island. The captain came up to the bridge at 1235 looking for an ETA for Crooked Island, which I estimated to be at 1400. I sighted the light tower at Bird Rock at about 1300 and we passed at 1408, 6.5 miles off, steering 200. There was not much to see, but more than we had seen for the last two days. We continued on 200 for the rest of the watch. There are a few small islands south west of Crooked Island that we had to clear before turning southeast to round Cuba. We cleared the islands on the Dog Watch, while the second was below for dinner, and I changed the heading to 155 to set us well clear of Cuba.

When I relieved the third that night, the captain was on the bridge. Punta Maisi was visible broad on the starboard bow and the radar indicated 20 miles distant. The captain wanted positions every 20 minutes. At 0100 I altered our heading 3 degrees to port to compensate for the current pushing us west toward the point. At 0145, well past the point, I changed course to 209, heading through the Windward Passage and into the Caribbean Sea.

Chapter 4

South to Panama

Passage from the eastern point of Cuba to Cristobal, Panama takes about two days. I was on deck that morning, looking for fire stations and safety equipment. We passed Navassa Island to starboard at around 1100, about ten miles off. Navassa Island is one of those odd ball islands that every one claims but no one uses. It's claimed by the U.S. now and shows up that way on our charts, but it's also claimed by some Colombian outfit, Jamaica and Haiti, it's closest neighbor. It was mined for some sort of fertilizer a century ago, but has been uninhabited for a long time now. As far as I know, there isn't any fresh water on the island and most of it is protected by 25-50 foot cliffs; not very inviting unless you're a lighthouse keeper. On the bridge, I tracked it for about an hour until it disappeared from radar and then used dead reckoning for the rest of the watch as there was no LORAN signal in that area.

When my normal business was completed (noon report, weather, etc.), I stepped through the starboard door and walked out on the bridge wing just beyond the windbreak. I leaned on the rail with the breeze in my face. The sun was bright and high, about 85 degrees, and bearing north. We had a lazy roll from long low swells, and the wind waves were starting to flatten and shimmered like a thousand mirrors scattered behind us. I watched the ship ride the swells, pushing the white foam from the bow wave down the side. Each time the bow would dip the foam would spread and the boiling sea came down the side of the ship.

I was exhausted. For the novice, just walking around on a ship is tiring. Your weight changes constantly with the ship movement (you weigh less as the ship plunges down and more as she surges up) and you are engaged in a continuous balancing act between the pitching and rolling. Add to that the number of times you are going up and down ladders and stairs, and that you never seem to get more than five hours sleep at a time (usually three to four). Then there is the chair issue. There is only one chair on the bridge – the captain's chair. A watch-standing officer never sits; whether he is on watch for four, six or eight hours, he stands his watch. For me, there was also the anxiety of a new world and of things to come. I hadn't even looked at cargo operations yet. Even so, at that particular moment, things looked good. From that view, from the bridge wing, the air was fresh; none of that oily, rusty steel smell. And, looking out at the sea, I couldn't see all the peeling paint and rust stains. Sometimes life is good. I ran my watch and navigated the ship. No one was looking over my shoulder, and I had two days to figure out the rest.

The captain was on the bridge at 1500 and I rang the general alarm at 1515 for a fire and boat drill. The second mate took the starboard lifeboat and the old third took the port boat. The covers were removed and the plugs were installed. Before launching, a brass cap is screwed down over the drain. The painters were led out (A painter, in this case, is a one inch diameter rope that is attached to a thwart in the boat and attached to the ship in a location from which the boat can be towed.) and boats were lowered to the embarkation deck, the place the crew gets on the boat. There seemed to be a bit of confusion at both boats and it was a half hour before they were both out. My only part in this was ringing the alarm and making the logbook entry. I made a note to check out the lifeboats in my spare time.

The second arrived a few minutes late due to the boat drill. I spent the hour before dinner relief checking over both lifeboats; I had to check them anyway – they were part of the safety equipment. Back on the bridge, I noticed the second had prepared his night's stars in advance. He had chosen the stars he would use, estimated their approximate altitudes and bearings, and listed their sidereal hour angles (angular distance west of Aries) and declinations (celestial latitude) so as to speed up the calculations. Earth coordinates are organized by latitude from the equator to the poles with the North Pole at the top, and longitude starting with the zero-meridian passing through Greenwich, England. The celestial sphere coordinates are organized by declination from the celestial equator toward and away from the North Star, and by hour angle starting with the zero-meridian passing through the vernal equinox or first point of Aries.

After another very good but still very quiet dinner I went up to the officer's lounge to see what was there. I picked out a book "The Egyptian" and started to read. At 2000 I went to my room for some sleep before watch, this time I took my shoes off.

"2315 Mate" was the call at the door.

"Okay, I'm up." I lied.

I put my shoes on and went out to the hall. Before opening the door to the tween decks, I stood still and listened for the voices, or wind or whatever but couldn't hear anything. So I opened the door and stepped through and down to the first step on the ladder. Closing the door behind me, I was in total black for a few moments until my eyes started to adjust. Again, I stopped, and listened – nothing, no voices, no wind, nothing.

It was a bright night with the moon and all, and though I was in the dark tween deck space, I could see pale blue light streaming through the door ports that led to the ladders that reached the main deck. I continued below to the main deck and through the watertight doors that led to the mess deck. The fare was lean that night, peanut butter on raisin bread. I hoped that the cook was sick or something, and this was not going to be considered standard fare. I found my way to the bridge a lot easier than I did the first night. And still, on the way up, at the tween deck door, there were no voices, or wind, or any other noise. Go figure.

Vich had no position for me, although by now, it wasn't a surprise. There was no electronic navigation in this area. "Vich" is what the old third wanted to be called, on account of his name. I didn't understand that because his name was Carl Rinkewicz; I don't know how he got Vich out of that. But I didn't care; I'd call him Spud if he wanted me to.

"290 – no traffic" is all he said as he shot down the ladder well.

I took a quick look at the chart in the red light; we were halfway across the Caribbean. Then I stepped through the door and on to the bridge. It was a beautiful night, the moon low in the west, the stars brilliant across the horizon. I verified the lack of traffic and the heading then went back to take a closer look at the chart. The second mate's stars were plotted, almost a pinpoint position, really sharp.

This was really amazing. I shipped out for the first time just one week ago and now, I was at the con of a tank ship, in the middle of the Caribbean Sea, in 2000 fathoms of water, hundreds of miles from anything headed for Panama. I went into the pantry and put a pot of coffee on. OS Galvan was on the port wing standing lookout; AB Rouk was steering. I checked the steering compass and standard compass against the board then checked the gyro repeaters on the wings and flying bridge. I checked the navigation lights, which were all functioning properly, the smoke tube system and the RPM indicator. After running out a four-hour dead reckoning position on the chart, I turned up the volume on the VHF radio and went out on the starboard wing to get some air.

I'd had been hearing the scuttlebutt for the last few days; the crew wasn't happy. The captain seemed amiable enough more of the time than not, and the crew didn't seemed to be over worked or overly burdened - the ship was quite lax. As a matter of fact I was really unimpressed with the professionalism of the crew and the care of the deck. As I had been thinking the crew was rather lazy, it seemed the problem was of an opposite nature. The captain gave no allotment for overtime. When a sailor is tied to a ship, he expects to be able to put his time to good use and work. He has eight hours of watch, eight hours of rest, and eight more hours to work overtime. He wants to work to make more money; he has nothing else to do. This captain was stingy with the money and allowed no overtime. So while the captain looked good to the company for saving money, the ship looked like hell and the crew was looking for a way to get off as soon as possible. There was rust and peeling paint everywhere; deck gear was scattered about; equipment was in various states of disrepair. So the problem wasn't the crew, it was the captain; and I guess that makes sense. The ultimate success or failure of a voyage rests with the captain.

I went back into the wheelhouse and called Parle who was on standby in the crew's mess to ask him to bring up some milk when he came up for watch. In the pantry, I poured a cup of coffee and drank it black. When Parle brought the milk up, I found it sour and had to toss it. We were too far out for fresh milk. The second cup was black also – and burnt. I went back out on the wing with my black, burnt coffee. The moon set at about 0300 and by 0315 the sea was black. What a view. The whole celestial dome was visible and the stars were brilliant. I saw meteors occasionally streak across the sky; probably not visible back ashore with the haze of pollution and the light scatter from towns.

"Still on 209?" asked the second mate. He had come alongside very quietly.

"209 she is." I replied, wondering how long he had been standing there.

"Any traffic?"

"Not one all morning" I responded.

"I've got it. Go below and get some sleep."

I went back to the chart room, filled out the log and went below for a snack.

As I stepped through the hall door and down onto the ladder to the tween deck I paused momentarily to listen, but heard nothing. I climbed down to the main deck, went aft through the watertight door and entered the mess hall. There was less to eat than before. I opened a new box of grape nuts and poured them into a bowl. Just as I was adding some of that fake milk, I noticed that some of the grape nuts were moving. Weevils! Weevils had hatched in the grape nuts! I opened another box, more weevils.

How long had those boxes been on the ship? I had no snack that morning. I took the two boxes with me on the way back to my room and tossed them over the side when I got to the main deck. While approaching the tween deck ladder to the officer's deck passageway, I could hear the wind under that door again, it sounded like muffled conversation, and this time I could definitely hear voices, but when I opened the door; the hall was empty.

I was on deck at 0900 hunting down safety equipment. I had located and checked most of it. There were just a few outstanding stations to find.

Noon put us two hundred and sixty-four miles to arrival at Panama; we would be anchoring on the second mate's morning watch. I took two sun lines an hour apart and advanced LAN and the first sun line to the second at our estimated rate of speed. It was a good fix, but then again, it was a clear day and we were making a steady 14.2 knots. A perfect position is easy to get under perfect conditions. The swell had been diminishing and was very low; the wind waves were just ripples. The watch played out quietly, just the drone of the engines, and the occasional vibration from being light. Dinner relief was uneventful and dinner was quiet with no conversation.

I filled out the Safety Log after dinner and read for a while, turning in at 2000.

"211, one ship to port" growled the old third as he brushed by me to get to the ladder well.

"And good morning to you too" I said to the trail of settling dust. Vich always seemed to have a chip on his shoulder. In a week's time he hadn't said more than two words to me off watch, and not more than a half dozen on watch.

I took quick look at the chart before entering the wheelhouse.

"Two on the port, mate; one three points off the bow and the other one on the beam." called Galvan from the port side door. I grabbed my binoculars from the holder and stepped out on the port wing. The binoculars were a going away present from my brother - when I was considering working ashore and not shipping out, he told me that it would be a shame not to use a license that I worked so hard to get. That was one of those life-changing moments, and I think that conversation sealed my fate.

Off to the port, both were ships showing mast and range lights and going our way. After a half hour I could see their bearings closing; both would eventually pass us. While on the port wing, Galvan asked me about flying saucers. He seemed to think the meteors were flying saucers. I didn't even try to explain that one.

I turned over the watch with three ships in sight, about thirty-five miles offshore and fifty miles to Cristobol. I could already see light scatter ashore and there was traffic on the VHF radio, mostly in Spanish. I skipped my morning snack and retired.

A knock at the door woke me.

"1115 mate."

I went into my small bathroom and took a shower in my very narrow shower stall. I had this really weird feeling, like I was off balance or something, sort of like stepping off an airplane onto the tarmac. I dressed and opened the door – silence. That was it; there was no vibration, no roll, no noise of any kind. I went over and opened the blind. There it was – tropical Panama; we had anchored in Limon Bay.

Chapter 5

The Panama Canal

On the way down to lunch I stopped for a few moments on the main deck to take a look around. The quiet and stillness were a little disconcerting. We were at anchor in Limon Bay, a safe haven, protected from the Caribbean by breakwaters. It was hot, with no breeze and few clouds. I ducked inside for lunch. The waiter looked rather dour.

"What's up?" I queried.

"I hear there's no launch service." He responded.

"Is that unusual?"

"We're supposed to have launch service in port, but we never do."

"I'll see if I can find out why." I stated, not knowing where that would lead.

The ship's position was on the chart along with a note indicating the anchor bearings of various landmarks. The watch was boring, just checking the bearings every half hour to make sure we weren't dragging anchor (unlikely in a protected harbor). There were nine other ships anchored in our vicinity. I filled out the arrival slip with the tabulated data for the voyage. The VHF radio squawked away in a variety of languages but there were no messages for us. I stayed in the shade, outside the oven we used to call a wheelhouse. The air conditioning hadn't worked for a least a week, which was fine with a fifteen knot wind going through the bridge, but now, in the tropics under a high sun beating down on a steel box with a dark red roof, the thermometer was indicating one hundred and eighteen degrees.

When the second came up to pull out the canal charts, I asked about the launch problem. He said that the contract stated that when the ship was anchored in a safe port for more than 12 hours, the company would provide launch service for the crew at least every 4 hours. But on this ship, the captain refused because he said that we could be ordered at any time to go through the canal. I asked if that was likely and he replied "No". Canal transit was by convoy and we were scheduled three days out. I wondered who planned that.

By the end of that watch, there were twenty-seven ships anchored. The second mate said that with all the traffic and congestion, there was at least one collision a week here in Limon Bay. Many foreign ships have only one licensed officer on the ship, and some licensing programs leave a lot to be desired.

"Hey, by the way, slop chest at 1930." He added as I was leaving.

I stopped and turned around. "What?"

"1930, the slop chest will be opened."

"What's that?" I asked. I remembered the term, but couldn't place the meaning.

"You know, the ship's store. The captain will have it opened if you need anything."

"Like what?"

"Clothes, deodorant, toothpaste, stuff like that."

"Oh, okay" I went below.

At 1930 I went to find the slop chest; I hadn't asked the second where it was, and wandered around for fifteen minutes until I found someone to ask. It was a dark grubby room with no light in it, or at least no working light. There was a short line of the crew waiting to get served so I waited until they were all through.

"Hi Captain, I just wanted to see what you had in there."

"Well come on in and take a look." He opened the lower part of the door and I went in to see what was stocked. There wasn't much, and what there was, looked pretty old and grungy in that dim light. There were rubber boots, some dungarees, work shirts, cartons of cigarettes that looked like they were from WWII, a limited supply of toiletries, and other smaller items that I couldn't get a good look at.

"Thanks Captain" I said as I went out the door.

"Don't need anything today?" he asked as I was leaving.

"No thanks, I'm good." I went back to my room. The slop chest was opened every week, and I think the biggest seller was the cigarettes, sold by the carton.

I took my book up to watch that night. It was quiet, not much chatter on the radio. My crew was below in the mess hall. The main deck was lit with work lights; standard procedure for ships at anchor. There were over thirty-five ships in the area now, with their decks lit. I finished my book and had the log filled out before the second came up. I didn't bother with the mess hall that morning, just went directly to the lounge. I picked out another book, Lucifer's Hammer.

I surprised my waiter again the next morning. I wanted to be on deck early to start looking at the piping system. The BALTIMORE CANON had fifteen cargo tanks and two bunker (fuel) tanks. The deck was a maze of pipes and valves. The tanks were laid out three across and five from forward to aft with the bunker tanks aft of the cargo tanks. Each tank had a tank top; not the top of the tank, which would be the main deck, but an opening for access to the tank. The tank top was in the shape of a cylinder about four feet across and four feet high and had a top with a wheel to unlock it, and allow it to swing open. Inside was a ladder that went to the bottom of the tank. The top had a smaller opening about ten inches in diameter with a removable screen in it so we could look in the tank and measure the distance to the oil for gauging the ship, or measuring the amount of oil in the tanks.

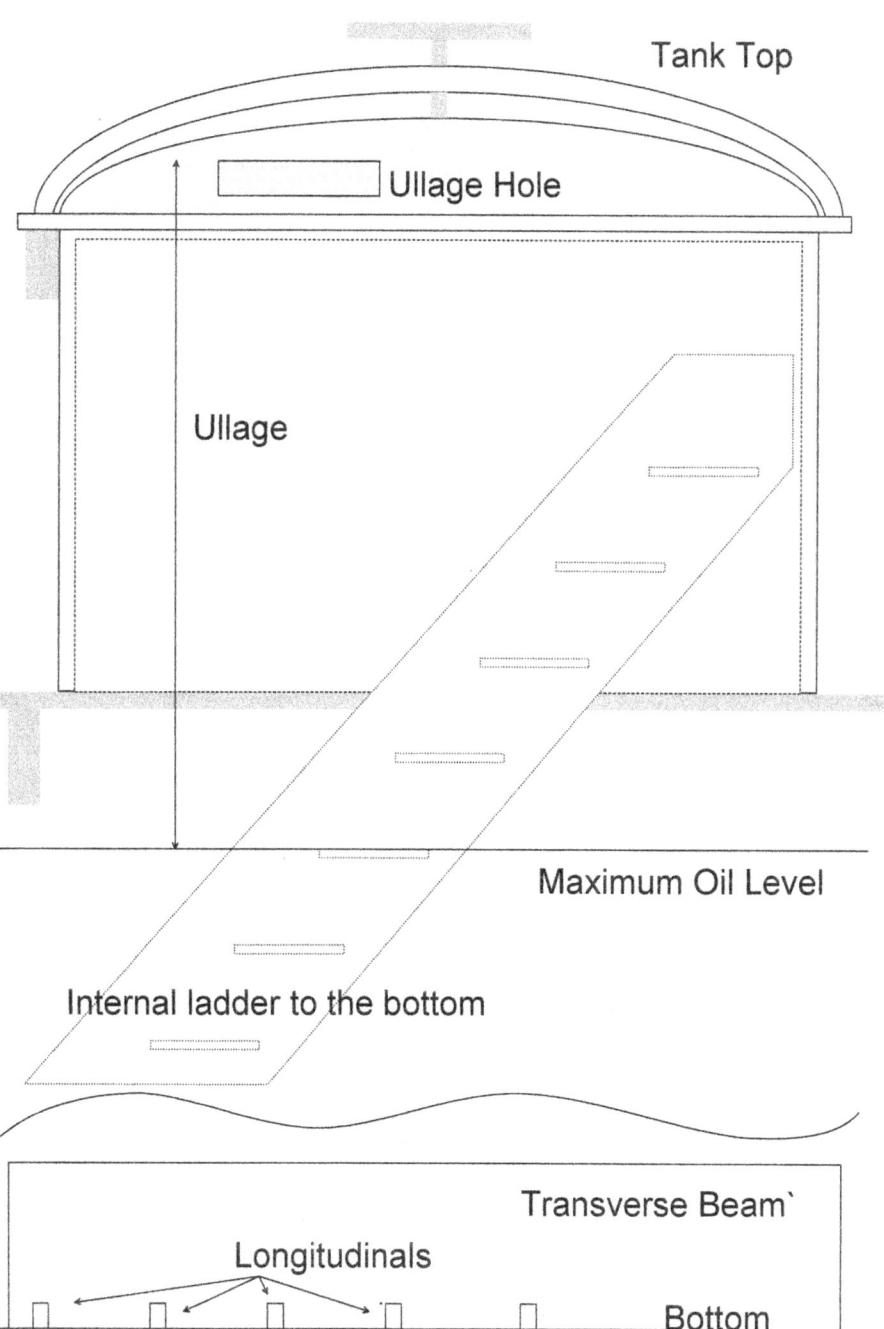

The distance from the tank top to the oil level is called the "ullage" and the tank tables are set up by ullage. It's a weird word; not my invention, someone else's.

There were four manifold pipes across the ship. Shore hoses would connect to these at the ship's side and they were connected to four deck pipes that went back to the pump room, each to a separate pump. There were also three main drop pipes from the deck lines used for filling the tanks. On the deck there were high and low suction valve wheels that controlled valves in the tank bottom lines for emptying out the ship. Valve wheels for starboard tanks were painted green, the port tank valves were red and center tank valves were half red and half green. Then, there were additional crossover valves, in pairs, painted white, allowing bottom lines to be served by different pumps (in case of pump failure). Bunker valve wheels were painted black. The pump room, aft of the cargo tanks but just forward of the main house, ran the complete width of the ship, and from the main deck to the ship's bottom, 50 feet below. That morning I started drawing pipe diagrams with valve locations. I needed to get to know this equipment for the upcoming cargo operations.

Anchor watch was dull. The only excitement was when the canal operator called to notify us that we had a transit time of 0800 the next morning. When the second took over, he told me he had to lay out charts for New Jersey.

But when he came back from dinner, he said the turn around port had been changed to Texas. Lately at dinner, the Chief Mate and 2nd Assistant Engineer would verbally assault each other from the time I entered the mess hall until they both left. But neither of them spoke to me; that was probably a good thing. Dinners were getting a little more animated, and I was being drawn into the conversations. I think my newness was wearing off. The captain sometimes spoke to me as an old hand to a new one; that made sense. The second mate and third assistant engineer were the only other officers that held conversation with me. With the rest, it was words of business or none at all. Overall, this was an improvement.

After dinner, a bad storm went through. Several of the ships, including ours, were hit by lightning; some more than once. It produced a unique sound when it hit the king post, something of a cross between a buzz, twang and the crack if a gun. I worked on my deck-piping plan after dinner, and finished it on watch the next morning. I made a note in my personal log to find a copy of the tank bottom lines so I could see how this whole thing worked.

At my 1115 call the ship was still strangely quiet. We should have been well on our way through the canal, but on opening the blind, I could see we were still at anchor. At 1505 the canal operator called and said the pilot was on the way. The captain came up at 1510 and I put the engines on standby at 1518. The pilot was aboard at 1535 and we weighed anchor at 1540 to begin our transit.

The Panama Canal is a waterway connecting the Caribbean Sea to the Pacific Ocean. You might think the canal runs west to the Pacific, but because of the shape of Panama and the geography of that narrow strip of land, the canal actually runs southeast to the Pacific. From sea level in Limon Bay, they raise ships about 85 feet to Gatun Lake in a series of three locks. Most of the canal transit is at that level including Gaillard Cut where they excavated through a 500-foot high ridge (what's left of the continental divide between North and South America). After passing through the cut, the ships are lowered to the Pacific through three more locks. The Panama Canal Zone is an area about ten miles wide and fifty miles long where the United States constructed the canal at the cost of about $400 million (in 1913), $80 million of which were buy outs and pay offs. This area was "given" to the United States by Panama, in gratitude for assistance in gaining its sovereignty from Columbia, to build and maintain the canal and to exercise governing authority in perpetuity; that means forever.

Our present situation might beg the question, "How and why did this marvel of American ingenuity end up back in the hands of the Panamanians (post northern Columbians), under the control of the Chinese?"

In most world ports, when a pilot comes aboard to assist with the transit of some waterway, he is only an advisor, but in the

Canal Zone he takes the con. The ship must maintain its place in the convoy and entry into the locks is a tedious business. Locomotives ride on rails on both sides of the locks and attach wire cables to the ship. The locomotives move along with the ships, controlling their movement in and between the locks.

The Gatun locks were each about 1000 feet long and 110 feet wide making the Gatun lock system over a mile long. At 1740 I relieved the second mate on the bridge so he could go aft with the crew to take on the locomotive lines. He returned at 1905 after letting the lines go, as we were exiting the Gatun lock system, and entering Gatun Lake.

I took the watch at 2348 as we were going through the last lock at Miraflores. We took departure at 0130 and headed south for our rendezvous with the BRITISH RENOWN, a British Petroleum supertanker in excess of 260,000 tons. That ship fit into the VLCC class (Very Large Crude Carrier). When I turned over the watch at 0348, we were still heading south in Parita Bay. The transit fee for the BALTIMORE CANON in ballast was over $10,000 and on the return trip in loaded condition would be over $40,000. Add that to the price of oil.

Under the control of the United States, the canal was meticulously cared for. The grounds were landscaped like gardens, the locks functioned flawlessly, locomotives (used to position the ships in the locks) were well greased and in good repair, and experienced pilots directed operations. This was not the case when I transited the canal several years later after control was taken over by the Panamanian Government. I couldn't believe things could go so bad in just a few years. The grounds were over run, there were locomotive breakdowns and several of the navigation lights were inoperable. But in those earlier days, we were moving oil, and all was well in the canal-zone. I don't recall ever thinking about the politics or the ownership.

The concern at the time was not the ownership of the canal, but of the oil we were moving. Public concern in America had to do with the oil being drilled in Prudhoe Bay, Alaska, and the pipeline built across that frozen land that carried it to Port Valdez just north of Prince William Sound. We were told that this was American oil and would be carried by American ships to American ports. But when we arrived in Parita Bay, we would be loading oil from a British Petroleum supertanker, to carry it eastward. Somehow the mass media was able to hide the fact that the oil in Prudhoe Bay was no longer American. British Petroleum had bought controlling interest of the Prudhoe Bay oil but gave the illusion that it was American by having American ships load in Port Valdez and carry it to Panama where it was loaded into one of two BP VLCCs, the *BRITISH RESOLUTION*, or the *BRITISH RENOWN*. After being gauged, the crude oil was transferred to an American ship like ours that would take it through the Panama Canal and deliver it to an American refinery. So, they sold our rights to our own oil, to a foreign nation and were buying it back one tanker at a time. For six months I ferried oil in this manner from British Petroleum to several American oil companies wondering how they could hide something so big. There was this big BP supertanker anchored in Partia Bay for years, with American ships on either side and no one seemed to notice. The thing was; American ownership was an American concern; not a Panamanian one. This operation was well off the coast of Panama, out of sight. And even if the Panamanians could see it, they wouldn't have cared.

But, sailors are simple folk; and as such, we had a simple job. Go over there; take the oil out of that tank and put it in your ship; bring it over here and put it in our tank; and don't get any in the water. That was a pretty well defined job and we knew in the end, if no oil went into the water, we did a good job. We didn't care whose oil it was, or who owned the tanks. We were all employed, they got their oil, and we got paid. Life is good – where to next? But, I'm getting ahead of myself. I had just made my first transit of the Panama Canal and as yet, had not seen the *BRITISH RENOWN*.

Chapter 6

Parita Bay

I took the noon watch, anchored off the *BRITISH RENOWN*, awaiting berthing instructions. The sun was high and bearing north; the sea calm with areas of small wavelets, and sunglasses were required. The *RENOWN*, about two miles off, was a beautiful sight, and the biggest ship I'd ever seen. She had a black hull with white rails, posts, masts and house, and a bright green deck; no rust on that one. At just over 1000 feet long and 160 wide, I guessed she drafted about 65 feet at 260,000 tons. She was engaged in berthing another tanker along her port side; and we were waiting for that operation to complete. The temperature on the bridge was 95 degrees. I walked out onto the port side wing to get some air. It was hot, stifling hot. I ducked into the shade. It didn't help much. I returned to the air-conditioned wheelhouse. 95 seemed cool after being outside. The engineers must have gotten the air conditioning to function.

There was no word for the rest of my watch or through dinner relief as to our berthing time, but my 2315 call spelled it out.

"2315 Mate, on deck, clear skies"

We had gone alongside while I slept. I put on my grubby clothes, stuck a note pad and pen in my pocket, tied on my knife and mirror, and dropped down below for a snack before taking the deck. Out on deck, I met Vich at #1 Center tank top, under the bright cargo lights.

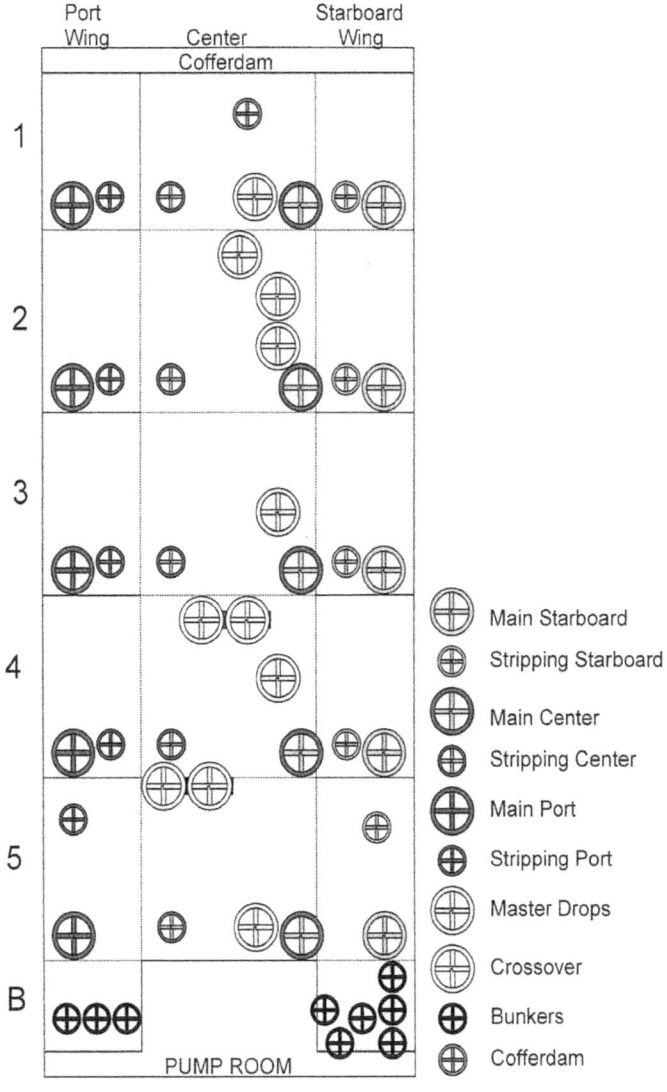

BALTIMORE CANON DECK VALVE WHEELS FOR BOTTOM VALVES

"We're stripping out this tank next." He growled as he handed me the radio and flashlight. We were de-ballasting. We had to get rid of all the seawater before we could load the cargo. We were pumping the oily seawater to the *RENOWN* for storage. I watched Vich go aft, then stood there alone for a few minutes waiting for something to happen; nothing did. So I found the valves for #1 Center tank and then went over to the tank top. I could hear the air being sucked through the screen at the ullage hole. I took out the screen and looked in with the flashlight, but all I could see was blackness as the suction pulled my hair toward the hole.

"Can you see the transverse yet?" The Chief mate had come up behind me.

"I can't see anything – I don't even know what to look for"

"Well, we're stripping out this tank next. I'll show you how we do it. The first thing you'll see is the transverse beam, when the ballast drops below it. It'll be shiny. That means we have about three feet left to go and you have to stand by the main valve. There are 17 turns on the main valve. If you hear the valve sucking air, close the main 5 turns. The next time you hear the suction, close it 5 more turns and open up the stripping valve. There are 21 turns on the stripping valve. Open it all the way and then close it 1 turn. Sometimes it jambs open if you open it too fast. If it jambs, use this valve bar to clear it. If the valve takes in too much air, we loose the pump and have to prime it; so you have to be on your toes."

Rouk was standing by the main valve waiting for instructions, while I watched and made notes. The officers don't operate valves; that's the deck hand's job. The crew didn't like it when you did something they were supposed to do; this was union environment and the rules had to be followed.

When the transverse frame showed, the Chief had me look in the tank. It was the structural framing running across the ship; I recognized it from course work at the academy. It looked to be about 12 inches wide at the top, and the light reflected off the surface.

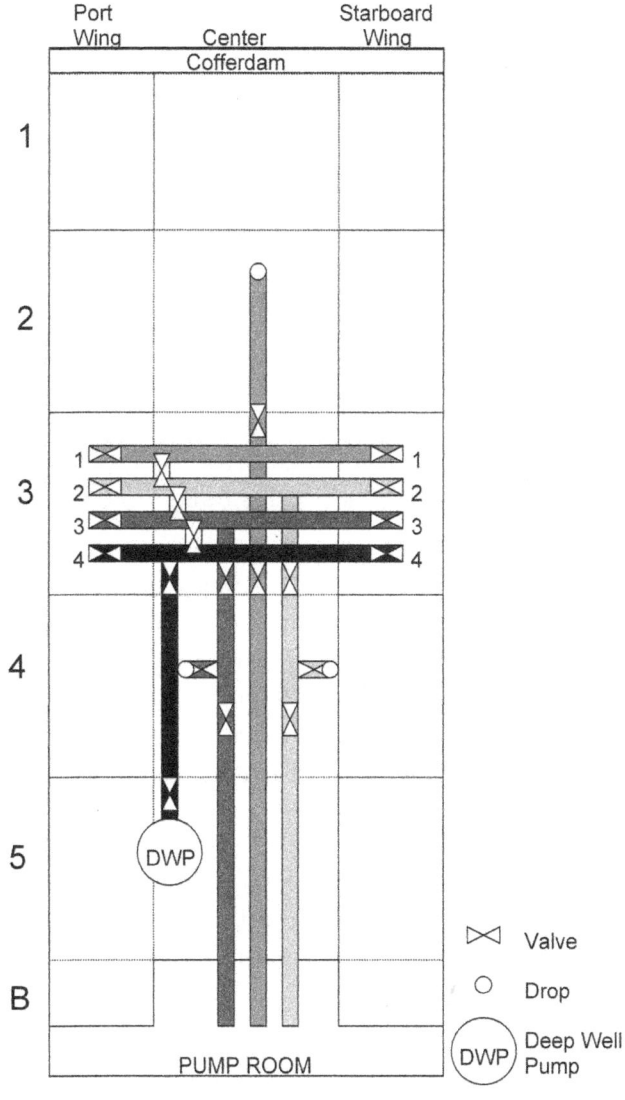

BALTIMORE CANON DECK CARGO PIPING

"The next thing you'll see is the longitudinals. When they show, there is only 9 inches left to the bottom." He explained.

About 10 minutes later I heard the first sounds of air being sucked into the valve.

"Close 5" The Chief ordered. Rouk closed the main 5 turns. Within 5 minutes he had Rouk close it another 5 turns and then open the low suction (stripping) valve. A few minutes later the Chief had the main closed another 5 turns and called the pumpman to have him open the main for #4 Center tank 3 turns. That was to give the pump enough fluid so it wouldn't cavitate but not enough to start gravitating back into #1 Center. When the main was closed completely I could see the longitudinals, and when the stripping valve was almost completely closed I could see the tank bottom showing and the last of the ballast being sucked out. I moved to #3 Center tank to try my hand. I only lost the pumps twice that night, as I dried out #3 and #4 Center tanks.

This was the first time I had worked with Simon Dwyer. Simon was one of those unforgettable types that you might read about in a paperback novel, but would never believe was real; that is unless you've traveled in the circles that such men travel, which most people don't. Simon Dwyer was about 65 years old, 5' 10", 280 pounds, and what little hair he had left, was gray and on the long side. Simon was a minister of the Mother Earth Church of Portland Oregon, husband to a girl half his age, lover of his mother in law, alcoholic, and Chief Mate on the *BALTIMORE CANON*. Oh, and I almost forgot, when ashore, he was also the proprietor of a half way house for recovering hippies long after the need. As Chief Mate on the first ship that I was contracted to, he was at least partly responsible for my abilities - or lack thereof - as a tanker mate, though I like to think he did a good job on my training.

Despite his notoriety, he was a very likable fellow, and he seemed to genuinely care for those whose paths he crossed; sometimes a bit too much, which was part of the reason he hit the juice so much. But in tanker operations, he was as smooth as they came. There could be no complaint on the speed, orderliness, or manner in which he loaded and unloaded the ship, always

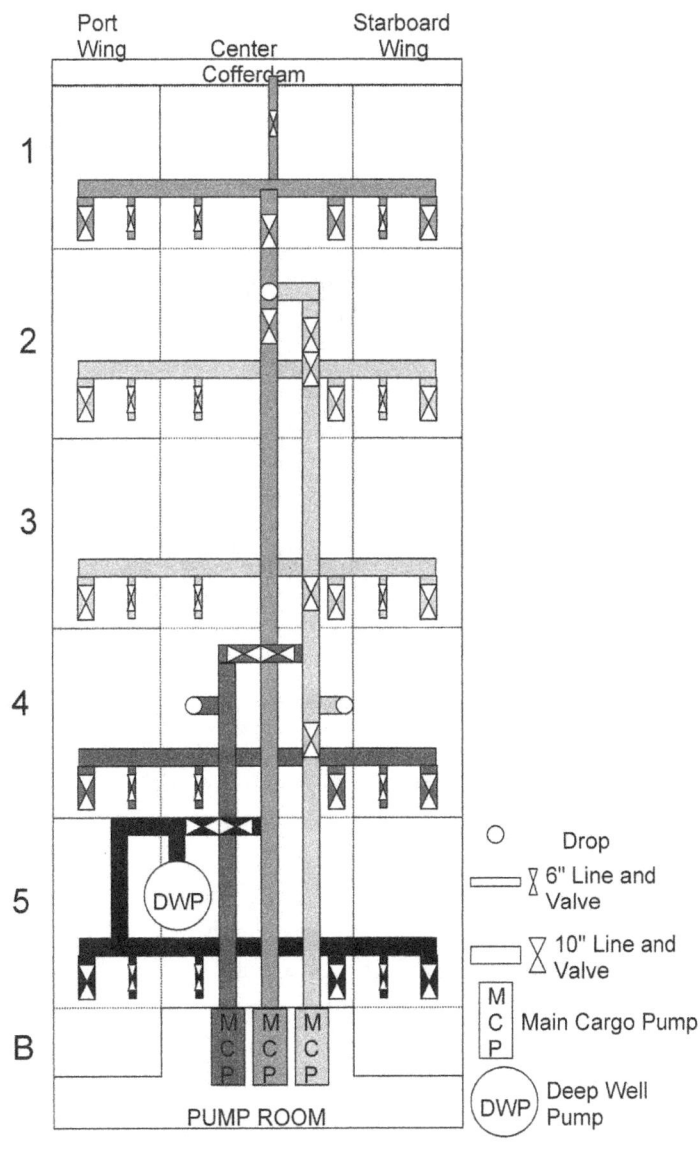

BALTIMORE CANON TANK CARGO PIPING

professional, always on time, and always complete. But, as experienced as he was, and as competent and thorough, a new order was coming that he would not fit into. Simon's days were numbered. Companies were petitioning the Coast Guard and unions to allow them to downsize crews and day working chief mates were going to have to start standing watches again. Many would retire rather than relearn navigation skills they hadn't used in decades.

When the second mate came on deck at 0350, we were still de-ballasting with only #5 Center to go. I turned over the radio and flashlight and went aft. We were high in the water yet the RENOWN was at least 20 feet higher though she carried cargo and we didn't. Between the ships were these huge bumpers that looked like they were 10 feet across and 15 feet long. We looked pretty small and shabby next to that British supertanker.

On the way to my room I stopped in the mess hall for something to eat; it had been replenished with fresh food in Cristobol. I felt a little odd leaving the deck with ballast operations in progress, and knowing we would soon start loading the cargo. I wanted to be part of the whole operation, not just bits and pieces.

On deck at noon, we were engaged in loading, and topped off a few tanks; #1 port, center, and starboard. I had to learn how to use the mirror to see in the tanks. The sun was bright and hot. Galvan wore his sneakers on deck and the soles got soft and were sticking to the deck, which was too hot to touch. Hard sole shoes are required on deck but Galvan, an Ordinary Seaman – the most inexperienced of deck hands - thought he would put his comfort above his safety. He paid for it with hot feet and trashed sneakers after one deck watch.

Oil fumes were blowing out of the ullage holes and as we closed tanks down the increased pressure at other tanks was lifting the brass screens. These screens were flame screens to prevent fire from passing from one side to the other, so we had to keep them in place, except to visually inspect the tank. To check the level in the tanks we had a tape measure with a float attached that we lowered to the surface. At a 4'10" ullage, or the fifth rung of the internal ladder we shut the tanks down. To do this, we had to remove the screen and use the mirror to reflect the sunlight into the tank. This method turned out to be far superior to the flashlight method as the sun provided ten times the light that the flashlight gave, except at night of course.

One of the problems in this operation was that I had to get my head over the ullage hole the see the level. Unlike the deballasting operation when fresh air is rushing into the tank, loading forces the hot oil fumes out of the tank making the area around the tank top non-life supporting. You can quickly get gassed, one good whiff of those fumes and the stars come out. It wasn't too bad loading once I got the hang of the mirror thing. But topping off tanks was a bit tougher. I had to spend a lot of time at the tank top looking in. And though I could hold my breath well enough, the fumes still got in my nose, and in my eyes. Looking into that 30 knot wind of noxious gas, I couldn't help but come away with a little of it each time.

At 1300 the RENOWN shut down cargo operations to gage us off. Some surveyors from Caleb Brett came aboard and took the ullage of each tank, and then lowered a brass bar, graduated with measurements and coated with a chemical to indicate any amount of water under the oil, to the bottom of the tank. While pulling the bar up, they pulled the cord through a rag held at the ullage hole to prevent the oil from getting all over us. The water was generally less than an inch, mostly just traces. I had to witness the gauging and testing as the ship's representative. By 1330 they started pumping again, and we were still loading at 1548 when I retired from the deck. I was burnt, I had worn a long sleeve shirt and my jeans but I had sunburn on my hands, neck and face. I was going to have to think of something else to wear. Jeans were too hot. My neck was burned so badly that the skin was hard and cracked. This was not going to do.

After dinner I tried out the laundry machines. I was running low on clean clothes and the machines were available. I found that crude oil stains don't come out. In retrospect I can state with authority that they don't ever come out.

Later I fished off the fantail, with the crew. The cook said he would cook anything we caught. We pulled in some good size tuna, and a few snapper.

By 2348 we were underway and in enough traffic (it looked like a fishing fleet) that I called the captain as the night orders required. By 0300 I was zigzagging through anchored ships, heading to Balboa. It was rather eerie steaming through miles of anchored ships that night. We were approaching the Balboa Anchorage when I turned over the watch. I went below for a snack and then hung out on the main deck for a while. We were low in the water and much more stable. The drone of the engine was muted and there was no vibration. The sound of the sea flowing down the side of the ship with the foam swirling and boiling, and fizzing was both closer and louder, as though I could reach out and touch it. Panama City's lights were in sight. The chief mate stepped through the door, talking on his radio.

"I'm going forward now Captain". The boatswain, Crowley, an AB from the 4-8 watch, and Levin, the 4-8 OS, followed the chief toward the bow. I could hear steam coming through the deck lines and the banging from the expansion of the steel. I walked forward along the rail on the starboard side to get a better view. The sky was getting lighter; sunrise was about a half hour off. Levin tested the anchor windlass brake to make sure it was on and Crowley and the boatswain released the chain pawl. A few minutes later Crowley took tension with the steam drive.

"Lower to the water" commanded the captain by radio.

Levin released the brake and Crowley lowered the anchor to the water.

"At the Water" returned the chief.

Levin tightened up the brake, and Crowley let some slack in the chain.

"Disengage the windlass." ordered the chief. Crowley disengaged the windlass steam drive. "We're ready, Captain." The chief called into his radio.

The ship had slowed but still had a slight headway. I felt the vibration as the engines were put astern, to stop the forward motion. The churn at the stern crept forward as the ship stopped and started to back.

"Let her go." squawked the radio.

"Let her go." called the chief.

Levin released the brake and the anchor chain leapt from the chain locker spewing rust, paint chips and dried mud, flying in an arc to the hawse pipe as the ten-ton anchor smashed into the sea. To give you an idea of the forces at work here, each of the links of the anchor chain weighted over 150 pounds at 18 inches in length and 12 inches wide. There can be no doubt that any ship within two miles of us, heard that anchor go out.

The ship was moving slightly astern and the backwash (churning water) of the screw (our thirty foot diameter propeller) had reached me. The chain stopped running when the anchor hit bottom but ran again for a few seconds as the ship backed. The vibration stopped as the engines were stopped. The brake was tightened and the chief looked for the chain markings to see how much had gone out. From then on it was just touch and go until he had what he wanted, and the ship settled in. While they secured the deck, I went aft. Sunrise was on us and I had a safety inspection to start.

The noon watch was at anchor awaiting transit orders. I stayed in the shade until the boat drill at 1515. Since we were at anchor, we lowered the boats to the water. Everything worked out fine.

At dinner we had fresh tuna steaks along with the normal fare. I guess cook meant it when he said he would cook anything we caught.

The midnight-watch was unremarkable; anchor bearings, reading, and foreign radio traffic. The word was that we would be heaving the anchor at 0515 to start our transit. I had been aboard two weeks at this point. I was no longer tired most of the time and I was starting to feel as though I belonged here on this ship with this crew.

We were on the northwest bound transit of the canal, in Gatun Lake, when I took the watch at 1148. At 1548 I stayed on the bridge for the second while he handled the stern lines in the Gatun Locks. Vich relieved me for dinner on the bridge. That was different, it was the first time someone relieved me on the bridge so I could go for dinner. We were clear of the locks by 1750 and I retired for the evening not yet knowing where we were bound.

Chapter 7

North to Yorktown

Vich was his usual curt self. I found us heading 029, 75 miles NNE of Cristobal on dead reckoning in the red light of the chartroom when I took the con for the midnight watch. Stepping through the door into the dark wheelhouse I could see blue light streaming through the portholes in the forward bulkhead. I checked the heading on the gyrocompass and the steering compass, and stepped out onto the bridge wing. The sky was clear with a very bright moon making it look almost like daytime. There was a fresh cool breeze, a welcome break from the stifling heat of Parita Bay. The freshened wind was raising wavelets, and the slight swell seemed to have no effect on us, sitting 39 feet down in the water; at more than twice our light draft. There was no Loran A or C in the area, and the water was over 1,500 fathoms (9,000 feet) deep, so this would be a slow watch; another welcome change from the hustle of the canal transits and cargo operations of the last few days. Haiti and Cuba lay two days ahead. My neck hurt from the burn of Parita Bay. I went into the pantry and soaked a rag, wrung it out and placed it over the back of my neck and on my shoulders.

Back in the chart room, the second mate had left the sailing plan on the chart table over the chronometer case; it looked like a five and a half day run to Marcus Hook, near Philadelphia at 13.5 knots. That sounded slow; we'd made better than 15 on the way down, with opposing currents. I opened the top chart drawer where the current voyage charts were kept and pulled out DMA charts 26001 for the Caribbean and 27005 for the Bahamas.

Our charts came from four main mapmakers; DMA – the Defense Mapping Agency (U.S. charts of foreign waters), H.O. – Hydrographic Office, NOAA – the National Oceanographic and Atmospheric Administration (U.S. Charts of U.S. waters), and Admiralty charts (British charts with the DECCA electronic navigation lines overlay. American charts might have an overlay of time delay lines for LORAN A, LORAN C or Omega.

The OMEGA system was based on eight transmitters located around the globe and gave an accuracy of about 4 miles under good conditions. The antennae were huge, some spanning valleys. Unfortunately it took several hours to tune in the system and due to the very low frequency range, the receivers would not maintain the signals in bad weather. The *Baltimore Canon* did not have one of these receivers and any OMEGA overlay charts aboard were purely accidental. The OMEGA system came to its end in the late 90s as the Global Positioning System leapt past it both accuracy and stability.

The track was already laid out on the voyage charts with the courses labeled. I studied them for a while. At 13.5 knots a four hour watch would cover 54 nautical miles so, I set the distance between the tips of my dividers to 54 miles by the scale at the side of the chart, and starting with the midnight dead reckoning position, walked off the watches along the track line with my dividers so I could see the areas that I would be at the con. There would be nothing ahead for the next two days but the deep blue sea. I put the voyage charts back in the drawer, then measured off 54 miles and plotted the 0400 DR position on the current chart.

There was porthole in the bulkhead to the right of the chart table at eye level. I opened it to get some air in the room. Underway, we kept the front portholes closed because of the wind, but this one was on the side behind the windbreak. At 0100 I filled out the 0600z weather report (we were 5 hours behind Greenwich and the reports are done every 6 hours at Greenwich time, also known as Z or Zulu time) and every half hour I checked the equipment; compasses and repeaters, navigation lights, smoke tubes, course recorder, rpm indicator, etc. The rest of the time I spent on the bridge wing, in the breeze, scanning the horizon.

The morning stars put us well behind the DR position, and my LAN and sun lines in the afternoon also fit that scenario. We weren't even making 13 knots. The swells had settled down but the wind waves had grown and we had spray coming over the bow. The spray was curling over both sides of the bow and soaking the fo'c'sle (forecastle). On the 1800z report, I classified the state at Force 4 on the Beaufort scale. I finished the safety inspection after watch.

By midnight, the LORAN signals were appearing, but were not strong enough or reliable enough to use. I fooled around with it for a while but it was just an exercise in futility. The seas continued to grow. I recorded 6-8 foot waves (considered to be moderate in open water), and overcast skies. Cuba was a day away; and it looked like I would have the watch for Cuba again.

There were no stars that morning due to cloud cover, so the last position on the chart was eighteen hours old when I got to the bridge just before noon. I turned on the LORAN and plotted the position. It was well behind of our dead reckoning. I completed the paperwork and sent the slips below. The captain came up to the bridge at about 1230 to look at the chart.

"Tom, we can't possibly be here at noon" he said, pointing to the position labeled on the chart.

"Captain, that's the first LORAN position I was able to get; but the LAN also aligns with it. I think it's good."

"But Tom, you have us making under 13 knots." He protested.

"But Captain, I can't help that; we are where we are." As I was responding, the captain was measuring off distance along the track on the chart.

"We must be here." He stated, pointing to a spot about twenty-five nautical miles ahead of where we actually were. "That's our noon position today; use that."

"Captain, you'll have us in port three days before we sight land." I explained.

"Mister, our charter speed is 13.5 knots, and we always make our charter speed; we'll tidy up with some bad weather later on." He explained, "This is where we were at noon – got it?"

"Yes sir, I'll make the adjustments."

So, apparently, the noon position report is not always an accurate depiction of the ship's situation, but more like a story that has to be told to bolster the reports of the negotiators at corporate conference tables.

Over the years, I've seen positions reported that were over a hundred miles away from actual locations. This may be why, in some cases, ships that are lost will never be found – they may be looking in the wrong places. Later on, the captain brought me a copy of the charter agreement.

"This is a copy of the charter; read it; take notes. I wouldn't want to have to fire you, but if you can't meet these requirements, you'll be looking for another job."

I read it thoroughly, and took notes. There were a lot of specifications; not just speed, but fuel consumption, cargo loading and discharge rates, conditions and exceptions etc. I got the gist of "we'll tidy up with some bad weather later on".

We rounded Cuba early in the morning in a lightning storm with seas washing over the deck; steering off the island, fighting the wind and seas. By noon we were trailing ourselves by almost 40 miles in the Bahamas. Shortly after that, off Castle Island, the LORAN A went down. I tried to set up and adjust the LORAN C, but wasn't sure it was accurate by the end of the watch.

I started up the LORAN C again at midnight; the signal was strong and steady. At 0115, about 68 miles ENE of San Salvadore Island, I saw a ship signal us by blinker light. I looked for the signal light key and found it but couldn't get it to work. I called the Master as per the night orders. The ship was bearing 196 at about 8.5 miles and I estimated its position to be 24 33N, 73 30 W. I tried signaling with a flashlight but they couldn't see it. The

VHF radio was on and monitoring channels 16 and 13 but no contact was attempted by radio. I could tell by the lights that the ship was headed toward us and the distance by radar was decreasing for a half hour. Then the ship left us. I observed it visually and on radar until it disappeared at about 18 miles distance. Before it was out of visual sight, I saw what could have been a white flare although it looked as though it was too high to have been fired from the ship, though it was below the cloud ceiling. I turned over the information with the watch at 0348.

The captain and radio operator were on the bridge the next afternoon, trying to fix the LORAN A unit (another exercise in futility). We were about one hundred and sixty miles off Great Abaco Island, by the sun and LORAN C, heading north. The boatswain came up to the bridge to hang a blackboard that had fallen, and in the process knocked a fan off the bulkhead and broke the glass and frame of the Station Bill (a document posted in several places throughout the ship identifying each crew members fire and boat stations and responsibilities). I think he cut himself but I couldn't be sure because he left rather quickly. The old third mate was the ship's doctor - he must have had some medical training. So, if the boatswain had cut himself, it would be in the old third mate's medical log – something I had no interest in.

I advanced the clocks the next morning to put us on Daylight Savings Time for the East Coast. The morning watch was a lot calmer than the afternoon watch had been.

It seemed strange – I had no night on this ship. I had a morning watch, an afternoon watch and daytime duties, but there didn't seem to be any night. My day started with the morning watch at midnight and ended at four in the morning. At about five, with the sun coming up I could get some sleep, sometimes six hours getting up for the noon watch, but more often only two hours because I would have other day time duties. I would then be on the bridge from noon until four, then be back at five for the dinner relief. After dinner I had inspections and paperwork to complete, retiring around nine for a few hours of shuteye before the callout just after eleven for the morning watch. I usually caught sleep in two or three hour chunks.

I noticed that the weather had picked up to force 6 when I took the noon watch. I hadn't noticed when I went down for lunch because the weather looked good; it still looked good when I went to the bridge for watch. In fact, I only first noticed when I took the con and Vich said "We're in Force 6 weather. No traffic." as he dropped down the ladder well. Force 6 weather meant 22-27 knot winds (which we didn't have) and 8-12 foot waves (which we didn't have either). It was also the break point at which we didn't have to make charter speed, or meet charter fuel consumption specifications. We actually had Force 4 weather, which according to the log, grew to Force 6 between 0700 and 0930 that morning. The noon position was already plotted showing a speed of 10.5 knots for the last two hours (about 60 nautical miles behind ourselves but starting to catch up). LAN wouldn't be until close to 1254 with the time change.

I went into the wheelhouse; Rouk was at the wheel on the gyro pilot, and Galvan was on the port wing. I stepped out on the port wing.

"Anything out there?"

"Nothing to report Mate."

I looked around. The sun was high, about 80 degrees bearing south, giving us a good view north.

"Hey Mate" Rouk called from the door. "The phone's ringing."

I slipped into the wheelhouse and picked up the sound powered handset.

"Bridge" I answered loudly with my hand cupped over the mouth bowl.

"Tom, the weather has picked up to Force 7 for the noon report." It was the captain.

"Yes sir. I'll note it in the log and on the slip." I responded. I didn't want to get fired from my first ship. I filled out the weather report (1200 on our new time). As all ship officers are certified weather reporters, I didn't find it very hard to fudge the whole report so it all lined up with Force 7 weather, 30 knot winds, 12-18 foot waves, cross swells from a moving storm center, the right type of clouds with the correct ceilings, wet and dry bulb temperatures, falling barometer etc. I hadn't known that my occupation would require me to be a fiction writer.

The captain came up at 1312 to check everything out and found it all satisfactory. Then he tried to get the signal light working, but couldn't. I found the hand held signal light in a locker behind the pantry; it didn't work either, the battery was dead. Steve the second mate, showed up at 1515 to check the chart. We'd been rerouted from Marcus Hook to Yorktown, Virginia. I got the idea that this was normal. He drew a new track and had me alter course a few degrees. Then he worked in the chartroom for the rest of my watch moving charts and marking books. He assumed the con at 1548.

We were still at Force 7 during dinner but back to force 6 by midnight, still behind, but not too far. Again, Vich just left me a DR position. I don't know what he had against the LORAN C, but I had to warm it up again to get a position. He always turned it off. Vich probably didn't understand these new electronic navigation tools, so he just ignored them. There were four ships in sight when I took the con and over thirty as I approached the cape. I logged Diamond Shoal abeam at 0314, 11.5 miles distant, and Hatteras abeam at 0355 with Steve on the bridge and in heavy traffic. A boat drill was scheduled for later in the morning so I left a note to wake me at 1000.

The boat drill went smoothly and was over in 20 minutes. That doesn't sound long but, they say, if you can't get the boats down in less than 10 minutes in good weather, when you're planning to, you won't get them down at all in bad weather. So you could say we still needed improvement.

After the boat drill, the captain opened the bank for the crew to get draws, that is, cash to go ashore with in Yorktown. I asked for a hundred in cash and arranged to wire the rest to my home bank. I had heard that shipping companies were notorious for not paying the crew so I had the money wired and figured I could have my father check to make sure it made it into the account. I had only been aboard for three weeks but there was no sense in loosing that.

We took arrival for Yorktown at noon. I forgot to ring it up and the captain was not pleased. I also forgot to have the pilot ladder brought in but was able to correct that without too much trouble. There were a lot of things to remember. I turned over the watch on deck at 1548 preparing to discharge the cargo, and retrieved the thirteen fire extinguishers that had to be recharged, and placed them by the gangway.

While on dinner relief, we had a situation arise. It seems, an oiler (an engine room counterpart to the deck side able body seaman) hit the third assistant engineer (an engine room counterpart to the deck side third mate) – intentionally – with the purpose of doing harm. The captain retrieved his handgun from the safe and went in pursuit with the chief mate. I can't remember what the outcome was as I was off duty before they caught him, but it probably was not good for the oiler.

Through the early morning watch we were engaged in continuous cargo discharge of all but #5 center tank, which we shut down at the half way mark. I asked Steve to give me a call at 0720 so I could catch the morning launch. The dock was a half-mile long and unsafe to walk on, so launch service was provided for shore leave. I hoped it was bigger than the one I boarded with.

The 0800 launch was a normal 32-passenger boat. There were a few guys returning that had left at midnight. The ship was getting lighter and higher as we discharged the cargo; and we had to lower the pilot ladder another two feet every two hours. By this time it was a long way down the pilot ladder, against the rusting hull. Most of the guys were dressed up, some in suits with dress shoes, climbing down the rope and wood ladder to the heaving launch which banged up against the ship in the 2 foot waves when it wasn't hanging 3 or 4 feet off. Nobody missed a step; they waited for the right moment to step aboard and none were embarrassed, including me, though I was worried.

We disembarked in a calmer area and got into waiting cabs to head into town. I should have gotten more money; the cab fare into Hampton was 20 bucks. I went to the New Market Mall area and wandered around until the stores opened. I picked up some film to record my first ship – should it prove to be something worth recording. I also picked up some stationary so I could write to my girlfriend (hopefully she still would be my girl when I returned in six months), to my father to give him instructions about the wires, and to send a post card to my little sister as I usually did from the various places I ended up. When finished, I got a cab to take me back to the dock; I had to make the 1140 launch to be on deck at 1148.

I was a few minutes late for watch arriving on deck at 1155. Vich looked a little impatient, but didn't say much; just that there was a technician working on the RADAR unit that was broken, and someone was inspecting the ship's radio. We were stripping out the tanks and completed cargo operations at 1500. Steve took the watch as we were inspecting tanks to prove dryness. At dinner relief, we were taking ballast.

They moved to an anchorage off Sewell's Point to wait for the bunker barge while I slept. On the bridge at midnight I was informed that someone stole the Captain's binoculars. I should have locked up the bridge when I secured it, though at the time, I didn't know we could lock the bridge. A tug and barge were approaching and I called the boatswain and my watch to the deck. Parle and Galvan showed up.

"Rouk missed the ship in Yorktown." Parle informed me.

"Who called Boats?" I asked

"I did" returned Parle," but I don't think he's coming. He's pretty stewed Mate. I couldn't even wake him."

"Well, that's a matter for later then. Let's secure the barge." I wasn't about to do a two hour call out for extra hands and delay the whole thing and I figured if anyone made a stink about an officer handling lines, both Rouk and the bo'sun would hang.

After taking the lines, and rigging the bunker hose, I set the two of them to bolting the hose and I went back to the mess hall and called the watch engineer to let him know his bunkers had arrived. Bunker C, the fuel of steamships, is a thick sticky oil, a residue from refining crude oil, that needs to be hot to flow. The barges usually have steam lines in them to keep the bunkers at least 140 degrees so they can pump them to the ship. The ship's engineers have to get it up to 600 degrees to burn. We burned 50 tons of this stuff a day, while underway.

By noon, the bunker barge had left and I was just taking anchor bearings. A letter was waiting for me on the bridge; postmarked July 10th, not bad, only 17 days to get to me. That would turn out to be typical, as the company would forward all mail to the next coastal port, rarely to Panama.

The letter was from my girlfriend, inquiring as to my whereabouts. She knew of course that I had departed and was on a ship, but that's too little information for someone romantically involved. My location would be of no use to her as I would be somewhere else by the time she got the reply but I sent it anyway, advising her that I would keep her posted when I was back in the states. She was still in college and had other things to keep her occupied during the summer. I didn't think she was on the edge of her seat waiting from word from me.

The pilot boarded at midnight and I started testing the gear at 0003. We started down river twenty minutes later and by 0200 the pilot had departed, we cleared the safety of Chesapeake Bay and I brought the head around to SSE rolling, pitching and vibrating toward Hatteras and the Gulf Stream; déjà vu.

Chapter 8

The Whistler

My 1115 call was on time and didn't require more than a one word response. I was practically pitched out of my rack as I put my legs over the side, covering the distance to the bulkhead in two giant steps. I cleaned up in my water closet (that's about the best description) wedged between the shower and the door frame to stay vertical. When finished, I stepped over the threshold and tumbled across the cabin as the ship pitched into a trough and slammed into a wave. I grabbed the bunk to help me get on my feet and pulled myself over to my desk to tighten the strap holding my chair down so I would have something firm to hang on to next to the locker. There was an adjustable strap, tying the bottom of the desk chair to an eyebolt in the deck. I kept it loose in good weather for better egress, tight in bad weather to keep me seated. The bathroom door was rattling with the vibration.

I worked my way down to the mess hall from grab rail to grab rail. The watertight door was secured and I had to time opening and closing it so I didn't get squashed in it. I was caught in the back with spray before I got in, and the deck inside was wet with a small bit of runoff seeping into the drain. In the mess hall, the tables were barren of their normal condiments and the table cloths had been soaked to keep everything from sliding off. I got my sleeves wet when I rested my forearms on the table, and I had to keep my feet wrapped around the chair legs to keep enough deck friction to keep me at the table. This was not a soup day. My lunch came one dish at a time, and I had him hold the drink until the end. There was a lot of noise coming from the galley; I could only imagine how they were managing. After lunch I worked my way back down the passageway to the main deck, exiting the house and climbing the ladder using both rails. I washed the salt off my face and hands before making for the bridge.

I relieved the watch in crossing traffic with a growl and a DR position from Vich. The ship's motion is most exaggerated at the bow and on the bridge, as those two positions are the farthest from the metacenter (a point between the center of buoyancy and center of gravity around which the ship swings). I worked my way out to the starboard wing and checked the traffic, then went back to the chart room to get a noon position from LORAN A, which had become operational.

I only had a few minutes to get it with the traffic situation. We were in the Gulf Stream and there were three ships on our starboard bow all heading north. I had taken bearings on all of them and had to take a second bearing to see how they would pass. The second bearings showed two of them passing well astern but the bearing of the third ship was not opening fast enough, so I stayed on the wing to be ready to maneuver if necessary. The third bearing was unchanged from the second indicating a collision course. He must have altered his heading to starboard. This was not good. The seas were from the south east about two points on our port bow and we were already rolling. The International Rules of the Road specify that the give way ship (that was us) should alter course early enough and significantly enough to be readily apparent visually to the other ship. I was going to have to alter course to SSW to go around his stern putting the seas just forward of our port beam and we were going to roll like a pig for a few minutes – during lunch. I wish I had thought to call the galley with this information.

The phone rang before I got to our temporary heading.

"Tom – What's happening?" It was the captain.

"I had to alter course for some traffic for a few minutes."

"You have to warn us for this. How long do you need?"

"About 10 minutes should do it."

"Ease her as soon as you can. "

"Yes Sir"

The pounding and shuddering ceased on our new heading but we were rolling over 10 degrees. That doesn't sound like much, but on the wing, near the house, I was moving 8 feet vertically with each roll. That would be about 15 feet at the end of the bridge wing, which I tried for about a minute.

I eased the heading a point at a time as the ship crossed ahead of us. We went under her stern at about a half-mile. I don't know which was worse, the pounding or rolling; but by 1300 the captain was on the bridge with the chief mate discussing the ballast and by 1400 we were taking on more. I recorded Force 6 with 18 foot seas on the weather report and the captain only added four miles to our distance for the day. By dinner we were lower in the water and riding easier with out the vibration. The spray was curling over the bow and blowing back to the house; which was about 500 feet back. I had to time my descent of the ladder to the main deck to keep dry.

As I stepped into the mess hall, and all eyes went to the door, before anyone could say anything, I threw my hands up in the air and announced, "Sorry about lunchtime guys." I figured I might as well get it out in the open, after all the best offence is a good defense. I'd rather they took their shots at me early and in the open than behind my back; and I think we were all better off for it. I also stepped into the galley and gave my apologies to the cooks. I think that event finally broke the ice. It was strange that I gained acceptance by screwing something up. After that dinner, I was on speaking terms with just about everyone – except Vich; that was a dead horse.

We were pounding again at midnight and it was a very dark night. I looked at the main deck from the tween deck and decided not to go for an evening snack. The waves were rolling down the side of the ship with the crests washing up on deck. The water was overflowing the fish plate (the steel of the hull that rises about 8 inches above the deck and keeps things from rolling off the deck). I recorded Force 8 weather, with rain, thunder and lightning. I guessed 20 feet for wave height, with seas washing the deck. The fore-deck was lit by the masthead light reflecting off the spray that was whipping up over the forward mast and blowing back and onto the bridge portholes. Other than the lightning, it was a pretty black night.

I was called at 0730 for breakfast. I thought that was a mistake but I got up any way, cleaned up and went down to breakfast. As we were still moving quite a bit, the tables had been watered. As a thought; this would be a good way to retrain people to keep their elbows off the table. Once again I got my sleeves soaked. The chief wanted me to start the safety inspection early and bring all the life rings in from the main deck before we lost any.

Walking on deck in that weather was a new experience. In the confines of the house, there are railings along all bulkheads in the rooms and passageways for stability but visually you are confined to the small area you are in without reference to anything external. Standing on the deck, watching the 600 foot ship move against the horizon, feeling the buoyant and gravitational effects, watching the crew as they adjust their stance for the rolling and pitching keeping themselves vertical though the ship is not, and realizing that you, yourself are doing the same, is vastly different. And looking out at the immense ocean, seeing that the railing is the only thing between you and the ocean's 20 foot seas should you loose your balance, is one of those life changing experiences. You are in a hostile environment, one of the most hostile; an environment to which men are lost every day of every year. I knew this when I signed on. I knew it on the training ship. But on the training ship, I was a student, surrounded by others who carried the responsibility. Now –

"What's up there Mate?" It was Crowley, the 4-8 AB.

"Nothing, just lost in thought for a moment." I replied as I came back around. I was standing amidships with 4 life rings and signal lights on my arm.

"Beautiful, ain't it?" It was more of a statement than a question.

"Uh – Yeah" and then I added, "Most people can only dream of a stormy view from the Hatteras Canyon."

"Where's that Mate?"

"Uh – just - out here" I answered realizing Crowley had no idea where he was. To him this was simply – at sea. He had no idea how deep it was, how far from land we were or what was over the horizon. He didn't even know that the horizon was 12 miles off. Perspective has a lot to do with responsibility and knowledge, and Crowley didn't have much of either. He'd been sailing for better than 20 years; that was his life. I guessed that he sailed 11 months of the year and spent the 12th month looking for another ship. He knew little of navigation on the ocean, but could tell you how to navigate to the best bar in any coastal town in the northern hemisphere. His life at sea included the nightlife at hundreds of bars at scores of backwater ports on four continents.

I walked aft and stowed the rings in the tween deck and then went up the starboard side to collect the rings on that side. The weather was easier there, less wind and less spray. I could count the seconds from the time I heard the bow hit a wave to the time the spray reached me, about 4 seconds amidships. I had to change into dry clothes and wash the salt off my face and hands before watch.

On the bridge, the captain didn't need to fudge the mileage for the day as the weather allowed for poor performance, but he did have me call the engine room and tell them that they were smoking heavily. Smoking means there was thick black smoke coming out of the stack when the exhaust should be clear. The second engineer, who was my partner in the engine room, was not pleased with our observation and let me know that with a few choice words. I let him have his tirade and begged off as graciously as I could under the circumstances.

Perspective – something an officer has to always keep in mind. From the engineer's perspective, the ship stops at the engine room doors. He lives and breathes the engine, and necessarily so. The steam plants are so complicated in their operation and maintenance under the best of conditions that when those conditions do not exist, it's a challenge to keep underway without doing damage to the system. A steam plant must be monitored and adjusted continually, by men working on steel grates, wet with the steam from the engine room and oily from all the machinery. They live in a totally man made environment devoid of anything natural and extremely hazardous to their health and safety.

A deck officer's perspective must take into consideration the ships loaded or ballasted condition affecting handling, the engine condition and performance, traffic in the vicinity, the depth of the waters transited, ocean currents, the prevailing weather conditions, the location of the ship at all times and how to proceed to the destination. With all of these considerations, his paramount concern is the safety of the crew, ship, and cargo – in that order.

There can be a friction between deck officers and engineering officers that is bred in the academies. It may be for competitive purposes or to give each a sense of value, but whatever the reason, it is detrimental to the safe operation of the ship. Deck cadets are trained to think engineers are nothing more than bilge rats with knowledge only of oil and fire and no conception of the restrictions and conditions in which the ship must operate. Engineering cadets are taught that deck cadets lack any intelligence whatever because if they had any, they would be engineers; as if all students were evaluated on entry, and the intelligent ones were sent to engineering and the dumb ones were allowed the run the entire ship. Unfortunately, there are many graduates that carry these ideas into the business and never seem to consider that neither could do the other's job, and that both are absolutely necessary.

Though many want the privileges, recognition and authority; few want the responsibility. In the end, it is the deck officer that controls the ship and also it is he that carries the responsibility of the safe navigation and operation of the ship. Even a third mate, the least experienced deck officer, carries the responsibility of the entire ship for the time he is at the con, on the bridge and this seems to bother the engineers. From the start, they were taught that they were smarter, yet by some twist of fate, they had to do the deck officer's bidding.

After watch I went below and put my two new bars of soap in the top desk drawer. I had finished Lucifer's Hammer so I exchanged it in the lounge for a book titled The Deep. The weather had lessened, and the pounding had stopped but we were still moving around a bit. I spent a few minutes on the port log for Yorktown and then went up to the bridge for the Dog Watch. Steve had his stars set out just in case there was a break in the clouds, though I didn't know why since we were still tracking on LORAN A.

"Prime rib tonight" Steve told me when he returned from dinner.

"Again?" I asked. "This is like the 3rd or 4th time since I got on."

"We get prime rib once a week." He explained, smiling as though we had arrived at the good life.

That sounded good to me; I liked prime rib. But even something like prime rib can be over done. In the 26 weeks I was on the BALTIMORE CANON, I had prime rib 32 times (they threw in a few extras). I was so sick of prime rib by the time I got off that ship that I didn't eat it for years. As a matter of fact, in the last two decades, I've had prime rib exactly once; and when I tried it, I remembered why I don't order it.

On the morning watch we were approaching the Bahamas but not close enough to see anything. The weather was down to a Force 6 and the night orders specified that we would be in Force 6 weather until further notice. There was no traffic and I tracked on LORAN A with hourly positions. All in all, this was a quiet watch, a relaxing watch, a night in somewhat stormy weather with nothing going on, that I was finally relaxed and feeling like part of the ship. I'd been aboard just about a month, a little less maybe, with 5 months, or a little more, to go. I was holding my own, with a few bumps and mishaps, but nothing serious. It was a strange time in a strange place with strange people, and it seemed my old life was so far away. These sailors; Galvan, Parle, Crowley, Tomlin, Levin; They had complete trust in me to be able to handle anything that happened. They really believed that they were safe in my hands. They didn't seem to grasp the fact that I was new at this and was winging it. As far as they were concerned, I was the mate, and if they needed anything, the mate could get it, do it, be it, or whatever. It took a few years for me to catch up to those expectations.

This was to be the first of many strange nights. As I look back, it seems to have started here, in the Hatteras Canyon, on the edge of the Bermuda Triangle, approaching the Bahamas; a desolate place that few know of, and no one would recognize though many have passed through it. At about 0120, as I was looking over the chart in the red light, measuring off distance to see who would get Cuba, I had this feeling that someone was looking over my shoulder. I turned around but no one was there. I went over to the half wall that separated the chart room from the ladder well and looked over, but no one was there either. Then I looked in the Gyro Room, vacant also. I stepped into the wheelhouse and asked Parle if anyone came through the wheelhouse but he said no one had. I didn't give it much thought at the time; I hadn't actually heard anything, and – they do call it the ghost watch. But each time I went into the chart room that night, I searched the place before I got down to work.

At 0340 I was standing next to Galvan, who was at the wheel monitoring the gyro pilot. It was late in the watch and I was listening to the wind as it whistled through the voice tube that went up to the flying bridge. We were still in Force 6 weather with 25 knot winds added to the ship's headway of 15, making a 40 knot wind that was whistling all over the wheelhouse. Every so often, the whistling seemed to go into a tune for a few bars, and then continue on with the chaotic stream that the wind blows. We both noticed it. The longer we listened, the more tunes we heard, until there could be no doubt that someone was playing us. I pushed open the starboard door and leapt out onto the wing, spinning around just in time to see a shadow of a figure slipping down the back ladder of the flying bridge. I raced down the narrow passage leading behind the bridge house and confronted the culprit as he landed on the deck. It was Steve, the second mate, grinning from ear to ear. I busted out laughing.

"You got us, both of us." We walked back to the wheelhouse. Tomlin had already taken the wheel. I turned over the watch and headed back to the chart room to fill out the log. As I descended the ladder well, shaking my head, my last sight of him that night was as he stood looking over the chart, in the red glow of the lamp with that stupid grin on his face. Walking along in the dark tween deck space that morning a question lingered in the back of my mind. How did he get out of the chart room so fast at 0120.

Chapter 9

The Gulf of Mexico

On my 1115 call, I opened the blackout and saw seas somewhat diminished from the day before. It was still overcast with low clouds but looked dry. On the way down to lunch I noticed we had turned the corner and were heading SW by W with a good size swell, broad on the port beam. Lunch was more subdued, in the moderate roll, about five degrees but slow. I got my sleeves soaked again. I still had to keep my feet wrapped around the legs of the chair but at least nothing on the table was sliding and the coffee didn't tip.

We passed San Salvador and Rum Cay on the afternoon watch. The weather was about Force 5 although still recorded at 6. There was no traffic as we approached Crooked Island Passage, and the sea flattened considerably as we entered. We approached Cuba on the morning watch and I had to change course to port to keep outside the recommended fifteen-mile limit again. Steve got Cuba and the Windward Passage, and I got Haiti and Navassa Island on the next noon watch. Navassa Island looks a bit too uniform in composition to be completely natural, but it is, so it's probably just the view from the east that gives it that birthday cake appearance.

By midnight, south of Jamaica and back in open water, the rolling returned with a vengeance. The swells were two points abaft the port beam, about 25 foot in amplitude with a 15 second period, and the wind was on the starboard quarter. So the swells were rolling up under us from behind, giving us a slow 15-20 degree roll as they lifted the ship, stern first, and set it back down to be lifted by the next swell.

The LORAN signals were starting to fade which made them questionable so most of the watch was dead reckoning. The sky was partly cloudy; there might be morning stars.

As I plotted the 0400 DR position for the second mate, it felt like the hair on the back of my neck was standing. For the second time, I felt like someone was looking over my shoulder. I spun around, but no one was there. I checked the ladder well and gyro room; both were empty. I looked at the chronometer, 0122 hours. I passed Galvan on my way through the wheelhouse and stepped through the door to the port wing. Parle hadn't seen anyone. I walked around behind the bridge and went up the ladder to the flying bridge two steps at a time. No one was up there. I walked around the flying bridge looking below to the bridge deck and the exposed weather decks below that; all were dark, quiet, and empty. Was he at it again? Or was I just spooked?

I gave Steve the course and traffic report as I was going below. I didn't say anything about the earlier matter, but as I went below, I thought I could see just a hint of that stupid smile in the red light as he gazed at the chart.

The next day brought a heavy haze so there were no stars or sun lines. We held another Fire and Boat Drill but didn't lower the boats to the embarkation deck on account of the roll. That night I stayed on the starboard wing between 0110 and 0200 watching the wheelhouse. If Steve tried something, I'd certainly see it; but nothing happened.

We took arrival at Cristobal at 1300 the next day and anchored inside the breakwaters. On dinner relief, I hoisted the Pilot Flag H-6 and started testing gear. Vich took the bridge while Steve went below to handle lines. I went aft to watch the line handling from the house top above the stern deck, to get an idea of what I might have to do in the future. The ship's crew threw a manrope (a synthetic line about 1 inch in diameter) down to the men on the side of the lock as we entered. The dock crew made them fast to the eye splice of a 1½ inch steel cable that was attached to the railroad engines. Then the ship's crew took a few turns around the windlass (a steam driven drum with a flared top and bottom to keep the line from coming off) and one of the ABs lifted the control lever that turned the windlass while another pulled on the line, slacking it every few seconds to keep it in the middle of the drum. The eye was pulled through the chock (an opening at the edge of the deck used to lead lines through) and placed around one of the bitts. Once in place, the engine tightened up the line and assisted us with our positioning in the lock. We moved through the last three locks on the morning watch and headed south for our rendezvous with the BRITISH RESOLUTION, the British Petroleum tanker that had replaced the BRITISH RENOWN while we were north.

I took the noon watch on the bridge at anchor, awaiting instructions. A few minutes later, the Mate on the BRITISH RESOLUTION called me on the VHF and told me to start heaving anchor at 1345. I called the engine room at 1300 and asked for steam on deck at 1330 (The winches were all steam driven). I tested gear at 1335 and we started heaving the anchor at 1350. One of the tugs dropped off the docking master and we went alongside. I stayed on the bridge relaying engine orders and keeping the bell book, until "All Fast" and "Finished With Engines" (FWE) at 1655, then closed and locked the bridge, and retired for the evening. We finished de-ballast operations on the morning watch at 0300, (We had more ballast than normal due to the heavy seas, and couldn't start de-ballasting operations in the Canal Zone or Parita Bay.) and were waiting for the Caleb Brett surveyor to certify the tanks as dry before we would be allowed to start taking cargo. Loading operations started on the next watch.

We topped off all the wing tanks and started #1 and #5 center tanks on the afternoon watch, and completed loading after dinner. I was burnt again. I needed to find a solution to that sun. The next morning watch, that is the morning of the 5th, I had been aboard exactly one month. I had worked one cargo discharge, two cargo loadings, four canal transits, had prime rib for dinner five times, and had eight bars of soap that wouldn't fit in the bottom desk drawer. And although overtime was light on this ship, I had logged one hundred and thirty-five hours of overtime that first month. There were just five months and forty-two bars of soap to go.

That morning we also steamed north and anchored at the Balboa anchorage to await our northbound canal transit. By the end of the dog watch we had exited Gatun Locks at the north end and were heading north in the Caribbean with discharge orders for Freeport, Texas.

The next two days were kind of sketchy as far as navigation goes. The weather was overcast and rainy, and there was no reliable electronic navigation that we had equipment for in this region, the most treacherous region of the Caribbean. The eastern Caribbean is bounded by a chain of islands and shallows mostly steep to, and marked by lights or landmasses, but the western area seems to be mostly large masses just below the surface, resulting in areas difficult to place and maintain hazard lights. This area is so dangerous to navigate that the most effective navigational aids are shipwrecks that stand high on the reefs and make good RADAR targets.

We went northerly steering 349 to pass east of the Quito Sueno bank, a shallow area about twenty-five miles square marked by four wrecks that have a good RADAR appearance. A light was placed on an outcrop of rocks on this bank in the early 20th century and it is probably still the most dangerous light to maintain in the Caribbean. I think Steve rounded Quito Sueno on the evening of the 6th because I sighted the Farrell Rock's wreck on RADAR at 0200 on the 7th putting us well west of our track. There is a good record of the ships well west of their tracks on charts of this region, as most wrecks are on the eastern sides of the banks, driven there by the prevailing winds from the east and by the North Atlantic Equatorial current that flows westerly through the Caribbean. After noon that same day I was taking RADAR sights of Islas Santanilla which I shouldn't have been able to see; putting us well west of our track and making me wonder how Vich got by Explorer Shoal showing at 4 fathoms on the chart, while we needed 8. The next dangerous spot was the Misteriosa Bank at 6 fathoms deep. That would be on Steve's watch and it looked like we would pass well to the west of it.

We bounded through the Yucatan Channel on the morning of the 8th like a greyhound in the three-knot northerly current. There was no need to add bad weather on this trip; we were flying. We traveled north of the Bank of Campeche, a region up to one hundred and forty miles north of the Yucatan Peninsula that has many shallows and is too dangerous to traverse with spotty LORAN A signals. There are reports each year of newly found shallows far from land on this bank. With that in mind, we steamed a good one hundred and twenty miles into the Gulf of Mexico before turning northwest to Freeport.

The next afternoon we were in reduced visibility. That's a catch all term we use for heavy rain, snow, sleet, smoke, or in this case, fog. Our maximum speed in this weather is legally defined by, us being able to stop the ship in half the distance we can see, though I don't know if anyone actually slows down any more. With electronic navigation, RADAR, and the radiotelephone, we could practically see through the fog, and talk to anyone in the area whether we could see them or not. I say practically, because we couldn't see anything that didn't give a good RADAR reflection, and if the LORAN signals went screwy, we wouldn't know it. Also, at this time the radiotelephone didn't work, although I wasn't allowed to log it. If I logged it as nonworking, we would not be able to leave the next port until it was repaired. The captain wanted the option of having it repaired at the ship's convenience; he didn't want the ship delayed on account of it. At midnight it was working sporadically, which meant of course that it was working. As far as good RADAR reflections go, it was difficult to see anything under one hundred feet long with a wood or fiberglass hull, even with a good RADAR unit; the aftermarket RADAR reflectors that they sell to these boat owners work better as a drag. At best, we could pick these up at three miles, if the sea clutter didn't extend that far, and if they weren't in the shadow of the bow.

We could see the white masthead lights of these boats about four miles off, if their batteries were charged, and the weather was clear. Even so, in the dark, a single white light tells a small tale and it takes longer to figure out the direction of the boat that it takes to get to it. Add to that, the fact that it took us a mile to turn once we determined that we needed to turn and you might start to see why small boats disappear on the high seas. Single handed sailing on the high seas is like Russian roulette. If you are gambling that someone will see you, you will be wrong most of the time. There are many foreign ships that do not have a lookout posted, and others that don't even have a licensed officer on the bridge.

We were approaching the oil fields, and this was another eerie night on the bridge. Off in the distance I could see the lume of stack fires on oil rigs beyond the horizon as the fog dissipated. I got the feeling again, around 0120, that I was being watched in the chartroom, but couldn't find any one. Yet I just couldn't seem to shake the feeling. Later that morning, as I was filling out the log book in anticipation on the second mate relieving me, I got that feeling again, like someone was right at my shoulder. I spun around to the left, but no one was there. I checked the gyro room and staircase – both empty. I went back to sign the log, but the feeling was overpowering. I slowly turned to the right – Whoa! There was a face pressed up against the porthole glass staring at me less than 1 foot away.

"Steve! " I yelled as I jumped back. That clown, he got me again! Steve went forward and came in the starboard wheelhouse door. I was still shaking, and my scalp still itched when he entered the chart room.

"Anything out there?" he asked, still chuckling.

"No, the RADAR is still on, no traffic."

"Go on below and get some sleep."

"Yeah, like I can sleep now-"

As I descended the ladder well, I could see him looking over the chart in the red light – with that stupid grin on his face. A chill went up my spine. On my return from the mess hall that morning, I could hear the voices in the wind coming from under that dark doorway in the tween deck space. This time, I could actually hear the words..almost.

At 1218 on the 10th we took ARRIVAL at Freeport, Texas. This was not a big place; I think the ship was bigger than the town. The tugs came along side and pushed us up against the dock where we tied up. I had the gangway put over the side, the scupper plugs installed, the signs posted, placed 12 fire extinguishers next to the gangway to be recharged and had the bonding cable attached. The bonding cable is a ground to the dock and has to be installed before the cargo hoses, to dissipate any static charge between the ship and dock. Cargo operations started on Steve's watch.

That evening the ship closed articles. A ship operates under Ship's Articles, an agreement between the Company, Captain, and Crew. The Articles can be for any term or voyage but are usually for a period of 12 months. During the Articles, the ship and crew are legally bound together by the terms set forth in the articles for the specified duration, although shipping unions have negotiated agreements and contracts that allow crew members to leave the ship after 4 months of service. It is rare to have a crew member, officer or captain on a ship for more than 6 months with the agreements in place today, but in the event of difficult or turbulent times, they can legally be held to the ship. A ship closes articles when the term has expired; and all crew members are paid their full wages and allowed to leave regardless of the time they've been aboard. That evening, everyone was paid in full, and went ashore, most to return for their next watch, some to go home.

At midnight we were engaged in continuous cargo discharge with fairly full tanks, so it was a slow watch. One of the 8-12 ABs, a guy called Bean Pot, came back around 0230, pretty well oiled. I didn't know is real name, all anyone ever called him was Bean Pot, or Bean. He was one of those guys that we couldn't get to wear shoes, on or off the ship. He decided to have a chat with me that morning about how he spent 300 dollars in Freeport that night and what a great place it was. I could hear a sizzling noise while he was ranting, and on looking down, noticed that he was standing on the hot steam pipe.

"Hey while you're talking, you might want to step off the steam pipe." I mentioned.

"Oh, yeah, sorry about that Mate." He replied as he looked down and stepped off the 8" smoking pipe.

"You burned you feet."

"Oh, that's ok Mate. I don't mind" he replied as he went on with his praise of the town, stepping back up on the pipe.

"Hey, you're standing on the pipe again."

"Sorry Mate." he answered, again stepping down, and continuing on about the town.

"You better go aft and get some sleep" I told him, and he took the advice. On the up side, he was half crocked so he probably only half felt it. On the down side, he was going to be sober in the morning.

Parle couldn't wake the baker that morning; he'd been ashore too.

I went ashore at 0750 and caught a cab to town for some shopping and a haircut. I don't know why it didn't occur to me to pack shorts and tee shirts for a ship going to the Caribbean, (though I was told the Mediterranean – same difference for weather) but it wasn't even on my radar. Freeport looked almost like one of those old ghost towns with old weather beaten buildings and a coating of dust settled on everything. Even the main drag was dirt. I don't recall seeing any tumbleweeds but I expected to.

I didn't find the barber shop in that dust bowl of a town but I did find a young woman who said she would be happy to cut my hair if I stopped by when she got off work at 3, after which we could go to the beach. I declined, as I would be on watch at that time.

I also found a very nice clothing store with two women attendants that helped me find shorts and shirts that matched, along with a white long sleeved cotton shirt, a pair of white lightweight painter's pants and some large white handkerchiefs. Then one of them escorted me to the dressing room, and volunteered to assist me in trying on the items. I declined that offer also as I didn't want to start any competition or jealousy between them. I found it odd that I was the only customer in a store with such attractive help and personal service.

I was back aboard in time for lunch, and relieved Vich on deck so he could check out Bean Pot's feet. It seems Bean Pot was complaining that his feet hurt and wanted the ship's doctor (Vich) to see if he could do anything for him. I don't think he had a clue as to the cause. As I wasn't required to tell everyone everything I knew, I kept my mouth shut and spent the afternoon stripping out tanks and wondering how Bean Pot was able to go through 300 bucks in a single night in that town. I also considered going back for that haircut, but as luck would have it, I had to stay on deck, after watch, to handle the bunker barge, and set the sailing board for that evening.

At midnight I tested gear, and we took departure from Freeport at 0130. I made the following note in my log that morning "If, in the near future, I get another chance to be in Freeport, I'll look forward to it. Even though it is a one horse town - with out the horse, and though it has few stores and fewer sights, it has a good beach that I'd like to try, and I look forward to the next time I may shop in their clothing store, for the help is excellent."

I don't believe I ever got the opportunity to return to that town.

Chapter 10

Dilapidated

Noon found us in the northwest Gulf of Mexico with clear skies, low swells and little wind, riding easy with a slight pitch and small slow roll of less than 2 degrees, but sitting high with a rhythmic vibration. We were in light ballast heading southeast to get around Banco de Campeche before heading south to the Yucatan Channel. The noon report showed us doing over fifteen knots, which made the captain happy and kept him off the bridge for the rest of the afternoon. The off-shore afternoon watch was a very pleasant watch. The crew had lunch, then took a siesta (since there was no overtime day work on deck) leaving me in peace on the bridge with a helmsman and lookout. By 1230 most of my work was done. An afternoon sun line, an azimuth and an estimated position (a DR position adjusted for current) were all that was left. I could spend most of the time on the wing, in the breeze, away from the peeled paint, and rusty smell of the house. I liked the 12-4 watch.

The midnight watch, in the central gulf, was rife with meteor showers above and some spectacular lightning off on the horizon to the southwest. The LORAN signals were strong in this region leaving plenty of time for reflection out on the bridge wing. We were headed for the Cuban coast. The Yucatan channel is about one hundred and ten miles wide but only half of that is available for deep draft ships staying outside of Cuban waters. The western side has a 2-3 ½ knot northerly current by the Yucatan Peninsula and the eastern side has a small ½ knot southeasterly countercurrent by Cuba. We rode the northerly current into the gulf and hoped to ride the countercurrent south about fifteen miles off the coast of Cuba.

I went into the pantry and got a cup of coffee. It was black and burnt and I had to add some water. When the watch shifted, the lookout would put a fresh pot on before going below. I took the burnt, watered down coffee out to the bridge wing to see if anything happened at 0120. Nothing happened.

A few minutes later I went over to the end of the wing and dumped out the coffee. That was a bad idea. First, the wing didn't extend out to the side of the ship so the coffee would have been dumped on the deck 35 feet below, and second, we were moving at 15 knots and the wind from this (that I couldn't feel behind the wind break) whipped the coffee like a fine mist over me, and the afterdeck. I remembered the wind as my arm was halfway through the arc and just a hair past the point of no return, allowing me to exacerbate the problem by trying to stop, bringing the bulk of the offensive matter onto the bridge wing, swirling around me. I went into the pantry and washed my face and hands before pouring a fresh cup of the good stuff. Then I went around to the chart room, looked around for any ne'er-do-wells, and plotted a 0200 position. I still could feel someone there, but there was no one. I turned over the watch at 0348 without incident, smelling of burnt coffee.

After watch and a snack I read a little in the lounge area then went back to my room. When I turned on the light, I saw a bug scurry under my desk. I got my flashlight and looked under there – a cockroach! Where'd that come from? I looked all over the room but didn't see any more. They don't usually come one at a time; I slept with the light on.

I turned out the light in my room and closed the blackout to make it dark while I was on the bridge for the noon watch. I wanted to see if I had a lone cockroach or there were more. By noon on the 13th we were closing in on Cuba but still a hundred miles off. Traffic was picking up but none of it was close enough to be of interest.

After watch, with much trepidation, I opened my door and turned on the light. I saw three of them running for cover. Crud, if I saw three, there had to be thirty; we had an infestation. I left the light on in the room after that.

My midnight watch of the 14th was in the Caribbean heading south to pass west of "Misteriosa Bank". We were shallow enough to go over it, but there was no sense in taking chances and finding a new shallower area to report. I recently looked at a chart of that area, and was amazed at the number and locations of shallows that have been discovered since I transited those waters. There are a half dozen places we could have touched bottom that were unknown when I was in those waters. "There but for the grace of God go I." The LORAN signals were no longer viable so there wasn't much to do; I just moved out a 0400 DR on the chart and had another cup of coffee out on the wing. I didn't sleep well that morning knowing there were cockroaches climbing around. I passed the word at lunch to see if any else had seen them; they had. The ship was infested.

I was back at the con at noon about twenty miles west of "Rosario Reefs" (southwest of "Misteriosa Bank") and turned it over to the second mate about fifteen miles northeast of Islas Santanilla, heading southeast toward the Gorda Bank. The midnight watch on the 15th was along the Gorda Bank with RADAR positions on the Farrell Rock's wreck, still heading southeast to get around the Quito Sueno Bank. We would round Quito Sueno on Steve's watch. The only marker at high tide (other than the four wrecks on the east side) is a light on the northern end, good for southbound traffic but no help at all for north bound; the 4 wrecks covered that approach.

We were about ninety miles from Cristobal at midnight on the 16th. This was another slow watch with no˙ electronic navigation or land aids. It was a relaxing watch with little to do. I spent very little time in the chartroom, just enough to put a 0400 DR position on the chart. I always seemed to get that uneasy feeling in the chart room around 0120, so I stayed out until I had to fill out the log. Steve was a little late that morning, or so I thought. I had finished the log entries and was waiting in the chart room, looking over the northern canal entrance chart when I could feel him watching me. I looked around and didn't see him at first. Then as I took another look over my left shoulder, I saw something in the shadows on the half wall by the ladder well. I couldn't quite make it out in the dim red light so I moved closer. It was a head, Steve's head. Steve was behind the half wall, and had his head sitting on the wall at a tilt so that it looked like it was just his head. I'm sure I jumped just a little as I realized what it was.

"How do you get in here so quietly?" I asked.

"You just seem to be thinking about other things." He replied.

"But, like at about 1:30, how do you get in and out so fast that I never see you?"

"What do you mean? I don't come up at 1:30. I don't mind getting up a few minutes early for a good joke but I'm not crazy."

"Well, if it's not you, then who?"

"I don't know. Check your watch out."

I let it go at that, and went below for something to eat. Then I finished reading "The Deep"; it wasn't so deep, I wouldn't recommend it. I picked out another book, "Below the Salt".

We took arrival at Panama at 0600 on the 16th of August and anchored inside the breakwaters; for another serene afternoon anchor watch in the light breeze, on the bridge wing with nothing to do but listen for the radio call with our transit time. It would have been idyllic had I been on a beach in the shade of one of those grass roofed shacks from which cool drinks flow, but I was at work, so the shade of the rusty, paint peeling bridge overhead, and ice water in a dirty coffee cup would have to do.

There was no launch service again, meaning no shore leave. There was some grumbling among the crew about this again, but the captain held his ground. Since we didn't have a transit time, we could be called at any time to get underway. I suspected that we had a transit time, but he was keeping it close to his vest so to speak. At midnight I got a cup of coffee and went out on the wing. It was another beautiful night. I leaned up against the end of the wing and looked toward shore, where the town was, and from where the cacophony of noise radiated.

Something caught my eye on the back rail of the wing. I slowly moved closer to get a better look. It looked like a huge green grasshopper. Wow! He was about four inches long. This was just what I needed. I put my coffee cup down on the leading edge and slowly moved toward the bug. It sat perfectly still. I reached up from below and grabbed it by its folded wings. Yes! I got it! I looked around quickly and everything looked okay so I ducked below with my prize and deposited it in my room on the dresser. Then I quietly closed the door and returned to the bridge. That should take care of the cockroaches. I named him the Geep. I know it was a weird name, but he was a weird bug. At 0112 the radio squawked.

"*BALTIMORE CANON*, Canal Zone."

I stepped into the wheelhouse and strode over to the radio. I picked up the receiver upside down, with the mouthpiece up, as was our custom. We used the handset like a microphone with our thumb on the transmit key, and listened to the speaker on the radio. This practice would cause me a lot of trouble when I was ashore between ships.

"*BALTIMORE CANON* back." I announced.

"*BALTIMORE CANON*, your pilot should arrive at 0200; plan to heave anchor at that time."

"This is the *BALTIMORE CANON*; we'll be ready."

"Canal Zone out."

"*BALTIMORE CANON* out." I notified the captain and chief mate first. Then called the engine room for steam on deck, first for the anchor windlass and then for lines, and gave them the transit time. I called my standby to have him put the pilot ladder over the side at 0145 and get to the bridge at 0200. Then I started to wake up the bridge. I turned on both RADAR units (only one worked but I started both any way because there was a rubber stamp for testing gear with which we stamped the log book and it had both units listed), then called the engine room to test the Engine Order Telegraph (EOT) and both gyro (electric) and telemoto (hydraulic) steering mechanisms.

The pilot, Paul Terrett, arrived at 0223 in a foul mood. After touring the bridge, he let me know exactly what his black thoughts were. There was very little visibility from the wheelhouse, three portholes was insufficient; and the wings were too short; they were supposed to extend out to the sides of the ship, he wouldn't be able to see how close to the sides of the locks we were. Then he got the captain uptight and the old man told me I wasn't doing my job because I didn't bring up a spoon for the coffee. We were preparing to move an 84' wide tanker through a 106' lock and he was yelling at a ship's officer about a spoon for his coffee – its no wonder the ship was rusting apart. Then the old man couldn't get any of his radios to work (he probably gave them the same attention as he gave the ship), so I had to find the bull horn and shout the orders for and aft from the bridge wing. Next he started to complain about the kingpost light being aimed toward the bridge like it'd been since they glued that tub together seven years earlier. He could have had that problem fixed at any time, if he would have signed the overtime for the crew to reposition it. Then we couldn't get a hold of the stand-by because the radios didn't work, so I had to take the wheel while my helmsman ran errands. This was quite the interesting watch. All of the canal pilots that I had observed previously had been cordial, and accommodating, but Terrett was neither. I guessed he had been drinking. There was something about his manner, and drinking sometimes makes a person short tempered. After all, none of us designed or built the ship; and I've seen many ships transit the canal since then, in poorer condition and with a worse design than the BC. There was no reason to go off on us for the design deficiencies, and he should have known that. And as for the captain, he was his own undoing. He let Terrett fluster him, and his other troubles that night were caused by his own niggardliness. Looking back, that was just a prelude to what was coming in the near future. You can only cut so much before progress is totally halted, and catastrophic failure doesn't usually give much warning. We had trouble with just about everything on that ship, and it usually had to do with a lack of maintenance, or a failure to replace worn and unserviceable equipment.

I remained on the bridge that morning until 0430 when the second mate returned from working the stern lines in the Gatun Locks. I couldn't get out of there fast enough. Below, I stopped at my room, slowly opened the door and turned on the light. I didn't see any cockroaches; neither did I see any Geep. I went below for a snack, read for a while, and then sacked out. I still didn't sleep well. I didn't know how long it would take him to eat all the roaches, or if he even liked them; and a bug that big makes quite a racket flying around. It was as if I had opened helicopter pad. After that night, I didn't see another roach, so I guess he liked them.

I took bearings off mountaintops for the noon position while steaming south in Parita bay. I nearly ran over a fishing boat that decided to play chicken with me; the captain was not pleased. There was nothing I could do about it. I was traveling through a fishing fleet and one of the boats started up and ran across our bow about a quarter mile off. There was not enough time to slow down, and maneuvering was out of the question within the area of the fleet. We were very nervous during those 15 seconds that the boat was blocked from view by the bow. We were really at the mercy of someone who may have wanted a new boat. The captain advised me not to do that again. I think that just briefly the captain forgot that this dingy we were riding with questionable steering characteristics, was an eighth of a mile long.

We continued on south and maneuvered into position to pick up the pilot from the RESOLUTION for an immediate berth. I remained on the bridge after 1600 while tying up and eventually Vich relieved me on the bridge and I went forward to work the bow lines while the chief mate went aft for dinner, departing at 1830 to catch the last of the board, before retiring for the evening. I finished reading "Below The Salt", which was a very good book; Costain tells a good story. I chose another book "Gideon Planish" to start the next day.

The forward spring line parted with a snap at around 2 in the morning as I was stripping out tanks. I replaced it with a spare from the tween deck space but the spare looked weak also. I don't know why it parted; we were de-ballasting and there should have been less strain on the lines as we got further out of the water. I warned the Second when he came out to keep an eye on it. I couldn't find the Geep that morning and wondered if he got out when the BR cleaned the room, but in the dark he made his presence known.

I topped off the wing tanks on the afternoon watch, in my new sun proof outfit. I dressed all in white; light weight painters pants, long sleeve white shirt, white neckerchief, white gloves, sunglasses and white painted work boots. I was still hot but I didn't burn.

The forward spring was still a problem. It was under strong tension with strands fusing together when I took the deck watch, so I slacked it a bit and kept an eye on it. It was frayed in several areas and past its useful life; it should have been replaced, but we had nothing better. I retired from that watch un-burnt, but I still needed some light weight gloves and a better hat.

On the way north that night the RADAR was out (again) so I posted the lookout up at the bow. I called Flamenco Island to give them an ETA (Estimated Time of Arrival) at the sea buoy. We anchored at 0310 about fifty yards from the buoy; it looked like I could reach out and touch it. I'm surprised we didn't get fouled on its mooring. We entered the canal on the afternoon watch and I stayed late to get through the Pedro Miguel locks.

We departed Panama at 0254 on the morning of August 20th, heading north for Lake Charles, Louisiana.

Chapter 11

A New Friend

My Indian (Parle) told me he planned to get off in Lake Charles. He'd been aboard for eight months and had his time in. I made a note to tell the captain so he could put in for a replacement and arrange his payout. Steve was also getting off in Lake Charles with four months in. It sounded like we were going to change ten or more crew members. I think the lack of overtime work and the lack of shore time in Panama had a lot to do with it. I heard several of them ask Vich for medical slips to see a doctor in port. A successful discharge for medical reasons would guarantee them a paycheck ashore until they caught another ship or the BC closed articles in eleven months. They wouldn't all get one, but nothing ventured, nothing gained.

Sparks was on the bridge for most of the watch trying to fix the RADAR. This was just a waste of time; both these units were old, probably from the late fifties, well beyond their useful life. I know the captain figured that if he could just get one working a little, then he was covered but that's not the purpose of a piece of navigational equipment. It's supposed to work when you need it, not just to pass a requirement.

We were riding low in deep water and heading for Quito Sueno. It felt good riding a loaded ship, visibility over the bow was better, the vibration was gone, the wind and sea had less of an effect, and I had the feeling that we were actually doing something; we had a payload. We were also closer to the water on the main deck and the air coming off the ocean was clean. On the downside, there were a lot of shallow places ahead that could stop us.

We passed the light on Quito Sueno as I took over the watch at midnight on the 21st and I calculated the distance off by timed bearings with our actual speed. I was hoping Steve got stars that morning because without RADAR we would not see Farrell Rocks or the wreck (Gorda Bank has no lights) and we were now in the most dangerous waters. About this time, as I was studying the chart, I got that overwhelming feeling that I was being watched again. I looked around, but saw no one. My watch indicated 0122. I didn't believe in ghosts but a thought occurred to me, and I stepped about 18 inches to the right, turned slightly left, pointed to our position on the chart and said, "We're right in this area."

Within a couple of seconds, the feeling vanished, or more like evaporated. I felt alone, and at peace. That was weird. I closed my eyes and stood there for a few more seconds; I felt good, like I had just done someone a favor. I opened my eyes, put the pencil between the triangles so it wouldn't roll off the chart table, and walked into the wheelhouse. Everything seemed in order so I stepped out onto the starboard wing to wait for a fresh pot of coffee. I leaned against the end of the wing and looked back at the porthole to the chartroom with its dim red glow. Maybe there was someone there; maybe they call this the ghost watch for a reason. Maybe this guy always shows up at the same time. I planned to check the next morning. I didn't tell Steve when he came up; I didn't need any one thinking I was going nuts or something.

Down below, I couldn't find the Geep again; I was always afraid he'd get away or someone would kill him, and I'd have to deal with the roaches again. I started leaving the light on in my room because it was cool in there, and I thought the Geep might need some heat. So I left the light on with the shade down. I must have been the ticket, because that's where the Geep stayed after that.

The next night I went into the chart room at 0115 and put a 0122 position on the chart. We were just north of Misteriosa Bank heading for the Yucatan Channel. I was checking my watch about every 30 seconds, waiting for 0122. They say a watched pot never boils and a watched clock never strikes; and I'll say those last two minutes took forever to pass. But at 0122, I could feel him, close by. I looked around; there was no one in that chart room, but standing over that chart I could feel him so close, almost breathing down my neck. The chill started in my lower back and moved up my spine, then the hair on my neck was standing and my scalp started to itch. I looked over my shoulder, but there was no one there. So I stepped aside and pointed to the 0122 position and counted to myself ..1..2..3.. And it was gone! The feeling was gone, and I felt good.

Who was this? Why was he here? And, why didn't anyone know about him? I'd been aboard for about six weeks, and maybe I'd have found him sooner if I didn't have a goofy second mate playing jokes on me. How could they have this guy hanging out in the chartroom every night and not know about him.

I kept a personal log while aboard that ship, and every other ship I've sailed. I kept the log to make sure I had a true record of the events surrounding me so that if there was ever a question, I would have no doubt as to the truth of the matter, since the ships log was less than that. In my log there is an entry for the midnight watch on August 23 that reads as follows:

8/23 2350 On Watch, Traffic, LORAN A

My friend came up to the bridge, actually the chart room, to watch me work for a few minutes, then disappeared.

Comment: A man, first name John, middle aged, tall, dark glasses, black hair (or at least dark), parted in the middle, rather tall, wore business suits, <u>died</u>?? of a chest (upper chest) malady – who is he? Apparently attached, in some way, to me.

That's what I wrote exactly as I wrote it, including punctuation. I hadn't read that log in twenty-five years; and I don't remember him ever saying anything, though I do remember seeing him briefly. I still don't know who he was or why he was there, but he did help out on more than one occasion.

We were headed for Calcasieu Pass, traveling through oil rigs at noon on the 24th. There were hundreds of oil rigs moored out in the gulf, on station long enough to be located on nautical charts with traffic channels established through the fields to the oil refinery ports. The rig's positions could be used for navigation with some caution as some are occasionally moved. Lake Charles is a town, not a lake, and it is located twenty-five miles inland from the coast. Well, I guess there is a lake as well, but it's a small one, smaller than the town. Calcasieu Pass is a four-mile channel from the Gulf of Mexico to Calcasieu Lake. North of Calcasieu Lake is a narrow windy river that passes through a few ponds and eventually leads to the port of Lake Charles. The dock we tied up at was small, and I couldn't believe that such a narrow river could be that deep. We tied up, port side to, and started cargo operations as I came on deck at 2350.

An hour later, at 0045, we sprung a leak. One of the main cargo lines put out a small stream of oil that amounted to about fifteen gallons by the time we got the pumps shut down and the manifold valves closed. The scupper plugs mostly held tight but we lost a few ounces over the side from a leak in one of them. The dock manager called the Coast Guard who sent an officer to investigate, but the officer got to the ship two hours later, an hour after we had everything cleaned up and the pipe patched with a band clamp. He seemed good natured about the whole thing (probably because there was no sign of pollution) and gave us permission to continue operations. By 0348 everything was running smoothly. In my room, the Geep was in his home. I slept well knowing the room was bug free, well, except one, and his noisy flying about no longer bothered me.

At noon Vich handed me the radio and told me that the Coast Guard was aboard to check out the spill from last night, and inspect our lifeboats. While we were standing there a technician came aboard to work on the RADAR units. Vich took him up to the captain's office while I started looking in the tanks with my mirror. They were still high, but I closed down #3 Center,

The Baltimore Canon Heading South

Oil Rigs in the Gulf of Mexico

and #5 Center, to keep for stripping. Now that I knew what a band clamp was and what it was used for, I started noticing them all over the place. There must have been a hundred of these clamps on the main cargo lines; talk about courting disaster.

Late in the watch another technician came aboard to fix the radiotelephone. I was relieved by the new second mate, a guy by the name of Don Chamb. He looked like trouble from the start. He explained to me that he didn't want to get into anything, 'just do one trip and get off'. I wondered why he even got on; maybe it was a union deal, a temporary assignment until a replacement could be found. Then again, his plans may have changed when he stepped aboard, the BC wasn't much to look at and her looks were probably the best part of her.

When I took the deck at midnight things were going badly. The cargo discharge should have been completed by 2300. We couldn't get any suction because the priming tanks had been taken down too low too early. Someone must have opened them back up during the day. We shut down three of the pumps and opened the crossovers, using the one main pump and the deep well pump. We stripped out the tanks slowly and completed the operation at 0410, with the new second arriving on deck late, at 0415. The cargo surveyors had been waiting since 0350 to start their survey and now began with Don observing. On the way back to the house, I asked the chief mate if he would go over the cargo operations with me when we got back to sea so I could understand what went wrong and how to avoid it in the future. He was a pretty straight shooter, and I figured he would probably be well disposed to help me get a better handle on operations, as the purpose was for me to help him manage a quicker, smoother operation.

At noon, I noticed we were no longer at the dock but anchored in a very small basin taking on bunkers, they had shifted out there while I slept. Ballasting had been shut down to replace a four foot section of #4 Line, near the deep well pump that was leaking. We finished bunkers at 1355 and hoisted anchor at 1500. I turned over the watch to the new second, heading south in that narrow winding river. I went up to my room to clean up, and on opening the door I felt sick.

"No!" but yes they did. I could smell the insecticide; they had fumigated the rooms. The Geep was dead. There were no more roaches on the ship; there also was no Geep. I suppose it was necessary, but had I known, I would have put him outside. I was rather depressed the rest of that day.

I went down to the pump room with the chief mate at 1900 to line up and take on more ballast. I would have to go down there again in a few days to add to my piping diagrams.

On the midnight watch I passed through the last of the oil rigs with their burn off torches flaming thirty feet over the vent stacks, lighting up the fields like an eerie scene from Dante's Inferno. The traffic was moderate and disappeared totally an hour out of the field, with the flames diminishing in the distance, and disappearing as they fell below the horizon as though sinking into the sea. Once again I was in the dark with total strangers.

I had two new ABs and a new ordinary on my watch. The 12-4 watch usually gets the new crew members as it is the least liked of the watches. Most sailors like the 4-8 watch because it leaves them with 8 hours of daytime overtime, off watch, so they can make the most money. The 8-12 is favored next because the watch hours are the normal hours that people are awake anyway. The 12-4 is the most difficult. The morning watch is dark and quiet, and it's hard to stay awake. On the afternoon watch they have to watch their ship mates making extra money while they can't. They can work the morning shift but then they have to sleep in the evening when their ship mates are playing cards. Sailors don't usually move onto the 12-4 watch, they usually move off it at the first opportunity. On this morning, my company consisted of three strangers and a ghost passing through. What a crew? What a ship? And I asked for this? Actually, I didn't just ask for it; I went out of my way to get it. Who was it that said "A man should not rush to his own demise."?

The new second was on time and rather gruff about taking the watch. He should get along great with Vich, I'd like to stay up and see that change over. I finished reading "Gideon Planish" that morning (another good book) and moved on to "Human Destiny" by a guy named du Nouy.

We were in the central gulf in rain and reduced visibility from a tropical depression on the 27th, rolling and pitching moderately, riding high with an occasional shudder. The helmsman, James Winters had a vague resemblance to Icabod Crane; lean and lanky, and clothing like something you might find on a scarecrow. He arrived with no baggage other than what was in his pockets, in retrospect a premonition of the future. His raspy voice was the product of his heavy smoking, and his emphysema; and his unsteady pins were probably the result of his heavy drinking. He looked like he was on the verge of collapse and it was hard to believe that he got a "Fit for Duty" recommendation from the union doctor, then again they probably consider you fit for duty if you can walk through the doorway and find a chair.

He looked to be around 60 or 65 with a drawn face and gnarled hands, and he shuffled about looking for an ash tray. Not finding one, he used his shirt pocket. I put him on manual steering for 15 minutes and checked the steering recorder, or, tattle tale, as the sailors call it. He steered as well as any other sailor, better than most. In the next few days he would be nicknamed "The Preacher", by the crew, not so much for his theological knowledge for he had none, but because he looked like the kind of preacher you might read about in an old Sinclair Lewis novel. When Menendez (my other new AB) came up to relieve him, he shuffled over to the door, slowly, and carefully stepped over the threshold and shuffled back to the ladder well to descend.

Menendez claimed to be a Chicano from southern Texas. He was tall, heavy set, dark skinned and had long wavy black hair. When he took off his shirt I could see scars all over his back. He said they were from knife fights. I had him put the gyro on manual steering for a while. His steering was good also. Robel, the new ordinary was a small man of just about 80 years. He was a professional ordinary and had been sailing for over 60 years with no desire to advance. He liked life at sea and would in all likelihood die aboard a ship.. He'd stayed aboard ships as long as two years and rarely stayed ashore more than a month. He was one of the happiest sailors I've ever met.

The 28th was easy sailing southbound toward the eastern Yucatan Channel, off Cuba, with good LORAN A signals and clear skies but strong winds that whipped the spray over the ship making it necessary to keep the lookout on the starboard side with the port side door secure. My friend was in the chart room on the morning of the 29th south of the channel. I was getting used to him stopping by, but still not comfortable; I always got that shiver when he arrived. I would usually set a 0122 DR on the chart when I got there at midnight so if I wasn't in the chart room at the appointed time, maybe he would see it and go. I still don't know much about him, who he was, why he was there, and why, specifically he arrived at 0122.

It took about 24 hours to transit the shoal area from Misteriosa Bank to Quito Sueno and I checked the fathometer recorder frequently on my watches in this area to verify other navigational information. LORAN usually became unreliable about the time we entered this region, leaving RADAR as the best navigational tool. Fortunately, for the first time, both RADARs were now working. The alarm for the range light (the white light on the radar mast above the bridge) sounded in the afternoon and I passed word to the boatswain to replace it. Whenever one of these lights failed, the backup light seemed to fail also. I think someone was throwing the switch and not replacing the burned out bulb, so I always had to replace both.

Another curious situation arose. On the morning of the 30th, on our approach to Farrell Rocks, I stayed on the bridge until 0440 to show the new second how to start and set up the RADAR unit. He'd been aboard for four days, in the river, through oil rigs and off the coast of Cuba, and had not yet used the RADAR.

There is a frame by the bridge door where all licensed officers must post their licenses on joining the ship. I checked his license on the way out that morning – it was a Master's license. How did he get a Master's license without knowing how to set up a RADAR unit?

Chapter 12

The Would Be Master

I rounded Quito Sueno on the 30th in the afternoon, a day from Cristobal. Don wanted me on the bridge for dinner relief at 1650, a little earlier than normal; and he stayed a little later than normal; that is, earlier and later than what was previously considered normal. It didn't make any difference to me what the times were, but it seemed to bug him. I think it bugged him that I didn't care.

When he relieved me on the bridge, he wanted me to stick around to talk for a while, though it was more like to listen to grievances. It seemed that he was not at all pleased with his position on the ship, nor was he pleased with the rest of the officers. He was upset with the master because the master treated him like the second mate he was supposed to replace even though he had a masters license. He was none too pleased with Vich because Vich told him how we worked port time, and a third mate shouldn't be telling the second mate anything, like how to work the RADAR for instance. Then there was a problem with the chief mate who expected him to work cargo. I was inclined to agree with the captain and the chief mate, as they were running things. In any event I didn't want to show favoritism, but it was damn hard to agree with everyone with such disparate and conflicting views. Such are the problems of the junior third mate. The solution – I just kept my mouth shut.

Don signed on as the second mate, but wanted to be treated like the captain. He should have waited for a captain's slot if that's what he wanted. Over the years, in tough times, I've known masters that signed on as third mates just to get a job. Regardless of your license, you do the job you signed on to do; you are what you signed on as, not what you're qualified for. Of course, that was easy for me, I was green and wasn't going to tell any one what to do. For now, it was back to Panama and the same old thing – or so I thought.

In the morning I got together with the Chief Mate and started documenting the cargo loading process. Loading was easier than unloading and since we were headed for a loading port, that was a good place to start. I had a note pad and took notes so I could go over things later.

We took arrival at Panama at 1530 on the 31st and anchored in the inner harbor. When I went up for dinner relief and asked Don what he was taking anchor bearings on, he cut me off gruffly with, "Oh we're not going anywhere." and went below for dinner. Okay, so he wasn't much for anchor bearings.

We made our next transit on the 1st of September. At noon we were in transit, southbound and the second mate relieved me on the bridge on time, even though we were heading into the Pedro Miguel Lock. At 1605 I was sent to the stern to handle lines! Normally the chief mate handles the bow lines and the second mate works the stern lines, the third mate remains on the bridge. For some unknown reason, Don was staying on the bridge and I was sent aft. Vich relieved me on the stern at 1800 to finish up in the Miraflores locks. Why wasn't the second mate on the stern?

By midnight we were anchored in Bahia Parita, and when Don relieved me and asked if I was taking anchor bearings, I gave him the same line he cut me off with the day before, "Oh we're not going anywhere." Well, that set him off. He wanted to know how the heck I knew that, and when did I decide that, and so on …and on…If I'd have thought of that response the previous day, maybe I could have used it on him. But any way, he kept on complaining, so the heck with it. I didn't tell him the bearings I was using. If he was going to cut me off and jump on me like that, he could find his own damn bearings.

He actually came up the bridge in a good mood on the morning of the 3rd. I didn't get that, but I enjoyed it. As it turned out, the *RESOLUTION* was being replaced by the *RENOWN* and we didn't weigh anchor until the morning of September 5th. I had been on board for two months. I wasn't tired at all. I felt like part of the ship. I wasn't dead, the ship hadn't sunk and I hadn't been fired. Was this great, or what? There were only four months, and thirty-four bars of soap to go. I wondered if I would ever see Panama up close and personal.

So, the morning of the 5th we tied up to the *RENOWN* and started to de-ballast. On the noon watch we finished that operation, gauged off and started cargo loading operations. At 1540 we sprung another leak in #4 cargo line, but got it patched and cleaned up without any one on the *RENOWN* noticing, so we didn't have to shut down and there were no delays. I made a note in my pad to make sure to have patches and tools on deck for fast repairs.

I accepted an invitation to dinner by the third mate of the *SS MARYLAND*, berthed on the other side of the *RENOWN*. I got to see a new ship in good shape, on which everything worked; another world from the one in which I lived. The *MARYLAND* was an 1100 foot VLCC (Very Large Crude Carrier) on the Alaskan run, and sat 65 feet down in the water when full. She was really a beautiful ship and gave me hope that there was better in store for me than that pile of scrap metal I was piloting. Going back was like going from a cruise ship to a garbage scow. Even my good clothes didn't compare to the white uniforms of the British Officers on the *RENOWN*, that I passed on the way back. I was out classed and out distanced and it was patently obvious to the casual observer. I skulked back to my flotsam like a bilge rat into the sewer. The view I'd been given just made my reality all the harsher to endure. All I needed to make the vision complete was a bottle of Ripple wine, and a shopping cart.

It was raining at midnight, and continued through the watch, as I topped off the tanks, getting gassed from the fumes of the hot oil blowing up my nose and laying about the ship in a noxious cloud. We finished later that morning and moved north to anchor outside of Balboa in the afternoon. At 0200 on the 7th we weighed anchor and started the canal transit. Don was angry because I didn't say good morning to him. Maybe he just wasn't a morning person. I was a little busy that morning as we approached Miraflores. Strangely, again, I was sent to the stern to handle lines for Miraflores and Pedro Miguel locks. I knocked off at 0625 and retired while we cruised through Gatun Lake.

We departed Cristobal at 1300 and headed north without orders. At 1200 on the 8th, just north of Quito Sueno we were diverted to St. Croix, Virgin Islands. We turned ENE and passed the wrecks on the north side of the Serrana Bank. I pulled out the charts for the remainder of the voyage and laid out the tracks.

I found Menendez sleeping on watch the next morning; he said he was sick so I sent him below. If he wasn't sick, he'd be hurting later on because his watch partners wouldn't stand for a slacker. In the afternoon I worked out the return trip to Cristobal and I went up to the bridge after dinner to take the stars for the second mate. I think Don had been sailing master and forgot how to do some things. I missed dinner on the 10th because I was on the bridge taking stars, but Tad left a dinner plate out for me. On the morning of the 11th, the third assistant engineer (3rd A/E) rang me on the sound powered phone and wanted to know if I could change watches in St. Croix so we could go ashore together. I told him I didn't know yet because the second mate was leaving and I might have to work 6 hours on and 6 hours off in port.

We arrived at St Croix at noon on the 11th but there was no berth available and the water was too deep to anchor so we drifted until the morning of the 12th. I took Don's watch on the bridge with Vich handling stern lines when we docked.

We started cargo at 1355 and the chief mate told me to go ashore, have a good time, and not worry about my watches, so I did what I was told and left with the 3rd A/E at 1415. I wanted to buy a few things to take home, so we got that out of the way first. Near the gangway a taxi was waiting, so we made use of it to get to Christiansted for the shopping. An hour or so later we were wandering about, and the same driver stopped us to see what we were looking for. As we were looking for a place to eat, and he knew of one, we got in and were promptly delivered to Captain Week's Bar and Restaurant.

  Captain Week's place was an open-air type building, basically a pole barn with a corrugated tin roof and a pebble floor. It was quite large, probably held ten or more tables and the open rafter space was 12 or 14 feet high with all kinds of junk (the kind that washes up on the beach) hanging in it. We sat at one of the tables far from the entrance and the waiter, our waiter, our taxi driver waiter, came over and asked us what we wanted. We started with some drinks of the alcoholic type with limes and looked over the menu. There was a lot of good food on the menu, so when he returned we ordered a half-dozen things from fried shrimp to cabbage. The drinks were gone before the food came so I went over to the bar to get a few more and noticed that the bartender was none other than our driver, waiter, now bartender. So he brought more drinks, and shortly after, he brought the food. It was all pretty good so we thought it would be a good place to hang out for the evening. A few hours later, after the fish, rice, chicken and what have you, we were getting dry and still had more to try on the menu so I went over to the kitchen to see what was cooking, and there was our driver, waiter…let's just call him 'our man', cooking over the grill. I went back to the table and waited for him to get around to us (it was getting busy) so we could put another order in.

  The place was about half filled and it was the dinner hour so there was a lot going on. The sun was setting, the decorative lanterns were lit, there was some kind of Caribbean or Calypso music playing to fill in the dead space and it was festive, although somewhat reserved. As we were enjoying the atmosphere with the rest of the tourists, two of the BC's sailors arrived, loudly, and in rare form. We picked up the menus and half hid ourselves from these hoodlums, dressed in their short shorts, shirtless and shoeless. They walked right up to a table that a young family was occupying, grabbed two empty chairs from a nearby table and plopped down at the table with them.

"Hey, how you guys do'in?" one of them started in. The father jerked back a bit and looked at the two of them like they were from another planet. The mother's mouth dropped open.

Then the other one started in. "We're from the big ship that docked today; yeah, we work on it. Hey, what ya eat'in? Is the food good here?"

Then the first one jumped in again." We're hungry, we're going to get something to eat too, mind if we join ya? Hey, where's the waiter?

We both looked at each other. "You know we're going to have to fix this." I stated.

"Yeah..I know." He grudgingly admitted. We dropped our menus.

"Hey Guys" I shouted across the space. "Over here" I commanded as I waved them over.

"Hey Mate, how ya do'in? " They yelled back as they got up. They made their excuses to their new friends; sorry but we have to go, that's our boss, we hope you don't mind, and similar apologies. On their way over I mouthed the word "Sorry" to the father and he mouthed "Thank You" back. So we were joined by these two Mobile bare foots for a while and they had some dinner, leaving long after the family had departed. The place eventually emptied out and we were alone, so our man stopped by and sat with us for a while. I think he was Captain Week or the owner or something; I don't remember exactly; things were getting a bit fuzzy at that point. We'd had too much to eat, and too much to drink. We were going to have to start on our way back before we forgot what island we were on. The last thing I remember was that Kevin got sick and I almost choked to death on one of Captain Week's sea stories. I don't know where he ended up, but I woke in the morning draped over a cargo pipe, fortuitously, one of the BC's cargo pipes. What a night.

We took on ballast on my afternoon watch, which ended at 1730 with the chief mate relieving me for dinner; that was different. Don had left the ship without a replacement and the chief mate was going to have to stand a bridge watch on the way back to Panama. This was not going to be good; the chief hadn't stood a watch in twenty-five years. This was kind of ridiculous when you think about it. The chief had to work on deck all day; and now he was going to be on overtime for an additional 8 hours to stand a watch that he would probably not be able to handle. It would make more sense to have the two third mates cover the watch. We were more current, the overtime would be cheaper, and no one would be working 16 hours a day. But I think the captain had a problem with additional overtime for the third mates.

All hands were called at 2030, and I was on the bridge with Vich aft. By 2200 we were on our way and I went below to clean up. The chief mate relieved me on the bridge at 0350, not exactly sober, or more accurately, it was amazing that he got up the stairs. I stayed on the bridge until he stabilized and I could see that there would be no stars due to cloud cover. I went below after telling him to call me if there was any traffic or he saw any lights. There were no shallows around, and from where I left him, there was nothing he could go aground on before Vich came up; not that Vich was a remedy for this situation.

The 14th was a day of poor visibility, overcast skies, rough seas and a veering wind. (A veering wind changes in direction to the right indicating that you are on the dangerous side of the storm and will have higher winds and seas.) Menendez was sea sick. We were running on the wild side of tropical storm Greta, sending in 3 hour weather reports in force 8-9 conditions. The seas were coming in on the starboard quarter and growing. I pulled in the life rings and stashed them up in the tween deck area before going to the bridge.

Vich just left a DR position. I checked the facsimile reports and it looked like we were chasing Greta and would cross behind her, hopefully before she turned hurricane. There were long low swells coming in from the north, and high, cresting waves from the north east. We were already rolling 8-10 degrees. The 8-12 Ordinary slipped and fell on the deck; he shouldn't have been running, or wearing sneakers on deck. He fell on the starboard side near #4 wing tank and bounced a few times before sliding into the bitt. There are no soft landings on a steel ship. They moved him into sick bay (we had a hospital room with all the necessary devices for sawbones type remedies). We were now down one officer and one crew member.

The 15th was like the 14th on steroids. By 0800 we were about twenty-one miles from the storm center, on the back side, in Force 10 weather and rolling twenty degrees giving us a forty degree swing. The weather had shifted and now came in on the port bow. The swells were broad on our port beam with a ten second period and we were smashing into twenty-eight foot wind waves on the port bow, sending the spray up over the bridge in the 60 knot winds. At times it got dark, and other times lightning flashed all around us; I didn't count the number of hits. Visibility was up to a mile when I could see past the bow, and the sea clutter on the RADAR went out five miles. I had the steering on manual as the auto pilot couldn't handle the ten degree swing. (The helmsman needed something to hang on to anyway.) I was hanging onto the dogs of the center porthole when I didn't have my face crammed into the RADAR shroud. I didn't know how they were keeping the water in the boilers down below. There's a sight glass to indicate the water level, and the engineer has to keep the water level in the middle of the glass. If he gets too much or too little, it just looks clear and he can't tell if it's too high or too low, and doesn't know how to fix it. That situation calls for an alarm. If it's too high, water goes through the turbine fans (that's bad); and if it's too low, the tubes start to burn up (just as bad). I was glad I wasn't an engineer.

Access to the mess deck from the main deck was out of the question but it was also accessible through an engineering space aft of the main house. It was the long way around and I still had to go outside to get to it, but at least it was in a somewhat protected area. We had sandwiches and fruit that day; there was no cooking.

For me, sleeping was also out of the question. Most racks (bunks, beds) on a ship are laid out fore and aft so when the rolling starts the occupier simply rolls with the ship. But mine was laid athwart ship, or across the ship, so in heavy rolling, I slid about 12 inches up and down. The sheet burn and head banging would be bad enough, but think about your stomach under such conditions.

By the 16th, Greta had blown herself into a hurricane, but our tracks had diverged and our weather was diminishing. The chief mate asked me to stay on the bridge to take stars for him if the clouds broke. We hadn't had an actual position in two days, and he hadn't worked stars in at least two decades. I had no problem with stars, it may be the second mate's job, but all third mates have to know how to do it. I couldn't sleep any way, so I stayed on the bridge.

Vich was upset when he found me on the bridge at 0750. When we have to cover a watch, we usually split it. I would stay two hours longer and he would come up two hours earlier. That way we both get overtime, and no one has to be on the bridge for 8 hours unnecessarily. Of course I didn't get paid for that time; no one was going to say anything to the captain about the chief needing help. So that storm blew over.

I finally got a couple of hours sleep before returning to the bridge to figure out what we were going to use for mileage since we did so poorly (justifiably in this case).

I had the dinner relief that evening and went back to work evening stars, retiring 10 minutes before Vich arrived. We took Arrival at Cristobal on the morning of the 17th anchoring inside the breakwaters and taking on a new second mate with the arrival of the customs and immigration officials. I went below and got FOUR solid hours of sleep. I thought this job would be getting easier but that last voyage was a tough one.

Chapter 13

Perth Amboy

Just after noon on the 17th we weighed anchor and entered the Gatun lock system during a squall, while Greta was blasting Quito Sueno at one hundred and five miles an hour as a Category 2 Hurricane. The Hondurans were in for a bit of a blow. As it turned out, the Belizians also got hammered while we headed south through the canal in relative calm and anchored by the *RESOLUTION*. We moved in and tied up the next afternoon, and finished de-ballasting on the morning of the 19th. I stayed on deck for a few minutes to get the new second situated and see if I could read him a little. He noticed that there was a lot to be done on the ship (no kidding). I left it to him to figure out how to get it all done.

I topped off the wing tanks and opened #1 and #5 centers in the afternoon. When Larry (the new second mate) came out, he told me that overtime in Panama was now the same as stateside. I didn't know what that meant, but Vich seemed to, and he disagreed. Regardless of what it was, I wasn't going anywhere; and as that was not one of the things I was responsible for, I stayed out of it. When I got up at 2330 we were already anchored off Balboa. Things were moving right along.

By the time I got to the bridge for noon on the 20th we were exiting the canal zone with orders to head north to the Exxon terminal at Baton Rouge, Louisiana. That would be interesting - Baton Rouge is a long way up the Mississippi from

New Orleans and has one of the biggest refineries in the country. Exxon had instituted new hiring practices a few years earlier and was having a rash of groundings and collisions. They didn't all make the Marine Transportation Safety Board's reports but word of mouth is fast in a small field. In the past, Exxon Corporation sent recruiters to the academies to hire the top 10 cadets each year for its ship's officers. Everyone wanted the Exxon job; it was the highest paying and carried the most prestige. But something happened in the mid 70s that changed the way they selected cadets. They were first selecting cadets with special qualifications or attributes, and going to the top students to fill any leftover slots. Exxon was so visible in the industry and at the academies that it was obvious that they were trying to fill quotas; and by this time the results were in – in the news. I didn't know if I was going to see anything unusual up there, but I thought it would certainly be worth the trip; maybe I'd run into an old classmate.

We passed the first set of wrecks on the afternoon of the 21st in a tamer Caribbean than we left the previous week, and I discovered a pinnacle on Misteriosa Bank the afternoon of the 22nd just after I discovered a new coffee maker in the pantry. Vibration was one clue, and it was verified by the fathometer recorder showing very little water under the ship. Thank God we weren't any deeper. If you're going to find a shallow spot, this is not the best way to go about it. I logged it and made a record to send in.

The next morning, I was in the chart room at the appointed time, though I had forgotten about it, and my friend came by to look things over. He kind of startled me because I hadn't felt him for a few days. I quickly measured out the distance and put the position on the chart making a brief apology for my forgetfulness. But he didn't leave, or at least I didn't think he left because I still had the feeling he was watching. So I looked at the chart again. Strangely, we were south of the Yucatan Channel but the track was toward the east, not west. Why wouldn't we be using the current? I opened the top chart drawer and pulled out the 411 chart of the gulf. The track was laid out around Cuba and up through the Straits of Florida to Hatteras! I reached over the chart and pulled the ship's log under the red light – we'd been diverted to Perth Amboy, New Jersey. I guess Vich forgot to pass on one of the details in his haste to get below. "Oh, right, okay, I got it." I said to no one in particular, and the phantom beside me. He left. I put the chart back. If one of the sailors heard me talking to that guy, I wouldn't be able to get any one to stand that watch with me. I was disappointed: I really wanted to see Baton Rouge. One other thing Vich failed to tell me was that our captain would be leaving us in Perth Amboy.

When Larry came up we talked for a while about cargo operations. I don't think he liked working cargo. I'm not sure he liked working at anything at all. He always seemed to be late - late for watch, late from dinner, late from lines…Late Larry. And he always seemed to have small jobs for everyone to do. Have this cleaned, have that scraped, get this polished…He was trying to get jobs done by the bridge watch so as not to incur overtime. The captain probably told him he could do anything he wanted as long as he didn't have to pay for it.

I had a problem with that. I needed my helmsman to watch the wheel and I needed my lookout to look out. I wasn't going to do their job so they could do maintenance and then get fired for not doing my job.

We rounded Cabo San Antonio, Cuba's west end in the afternoon of the 23rd making little speed. I don't know why Larry cut that close to the coast making us fight the counter current. We were going to need that Gulf Stream to pull us along. The air conditioning failed again on the afternoon of the 24th, luckily we were heading north to a cooler climate. It may not sound like something important, but air conditioning is extremely important on the bridge. It's required to keep the electronics from frying in the heat and humidity in tropical areas. Fortunately, we were already 18 degrees north of the suns declination and going further. The weather was stormy along the coast of Florida and I had the normal problem with this newer crew of keeping them awake in the early morning hours. We passed Hatteras in bad weather on the morning of the 26th, Chesapeake Bay in the afternoon, and Atlantic City on the morning of the 27th. We anchored off Perth Amboy for a few hours before shifting to the dock. Once secure at the dock, I packed a bag, and went home for the night, leaving seventeen CO2 fire extinguishers by the gangway to be recharged.

That was the only time, in my shipping career that I was able to go home briefly while signed on a ship. It was good to see everyone, but I couldn't sleep that night (I hadn't slept during those hours for two months). The trip back was okay until I was halfway up the gangway and caught the full view of that rusted, dented, sagging thing we called the BC. I had a thought, briefly, to turn around and pretend I didn't recognize it. But by now I knew it all too well, and besides, I'd been seen. The trip home wasn't really worth it. The anxiety about missing the ship hung over me the whole time; I was just too far from where I knew I should be.

I was back in time to strip all the tanks on the afternoon watch, and then go ashore with the 3rd A/E. We'd both survived the last time, so, what the hell, right? That evening was a little tamer than the night in St. Croix, as we both returned in watch-standing condition.

Our departure was delayed due to the absence of the radio operator who failed to return. (Maybe he tried to get home for a few hours too.) All American ships were required to carry a radio operator to operate the ships short wave radio. That radio was the only means of communication from ship to shore while at sea. The RO (Radio Operator), commonly called Sparks, transmitted, via Morse Code, all the ship's information back to the company as well as sent out messages for the crew and monitored emergency frequencies for ships in distress – more frequent an occurrence than you might believe. Our RO failed to return that night without giving notice. I met our new captain on the bridge as we prepared to leave the dock, a maneuver that was stalled while we waited for the RO. Eventually we moved out to an anchorage off Ambrose Light (at the entrance to New York Harbor) to await the replacement as there was no sense in paying dock fees while just waiting for a crew member. A new RO arrived at 1450 the next day, which isn't bad for trying to grab someone off the beach without warning, and we departed Ambrose at 1500. After watch I went to Spark's room and collected the personal effects of the missing RO, boxed them and posted the list on the captain's door.

About one hundred and forty miles south east of Cape Lookout, while crossing the Gulf Stream, the gyrocompass failed and I switched to telemoto steering by hand. I stayed on the bridge when the 2nd returned from dinner so he could work on the gyro but it still wasn't working when I left around 1900, nor was it working on the morning watch of October 1st. Larry was an hour late for watch that afternoon, arriving only five minutes before going to dinner. He laid the courses in close to Crooked Island this time and we passed Castle Island about three miles off, with the captain observing on the bridge. That was a little closer than we needed to be, particularly with one steering system down.

We steamed through the Windward Passage on the afternoon of the 3rd finding a pleasant Caribbean in weather sufficiently calm to hold a Fire and Boat Drill. Two days later we anchored outside the breakwaters in Panama with the gyro steering system temporarily repaired. That's right, two days later; that would make it the 5th of October. I had been on board for three months, and my tour was half over. A lot had happened in those three months. We had three crew members jump ship, we came to blows with a tropical storm, found a shallow spot without going aground, and then there was John, remember John? John was still hanging around in the early morning hours. I still hadn't told anyone aboard about John; I don't think I ever did.

On the afternoon watch of the 6th, we shifted our anchorage because we had drifted too close to the channel. Then the captain sent me below to type up a crew list for the canal papers. I knew they wanted the cargo manifest so they could figure out how much to charge us, but I didn't know why they needed the crew list if no one was going ashore. This would be my 9th transit of the canal and I still hadn't set foot in Panama. I could understand why the crew was upset. The three most important things to the crew were food, overtime, and port time. The first was fair to middling, but the other two were sorely lacking.

The trip through the canal went smoothly with everyone in their proper places, and we moved right in and tied up to the *RESOLUTION*. After "All Fast", we connected the bonding cable that the Brits lowered. The bonding cable is a heavy copper cable with a "C" clamp fixed to the end that attaches to the ship. It's a quick process and is the first connection after mooring lines. Then we had to hook up the cargo hoses.

The ship's manifold was made up of four 20-inch pipes running athwartships with gate valves at each side of the ship. The shore side, or in this case the RESOLUTION would lower 2 cargo hoses to the manifold drain pan, a 4 foot wide, 16 foot long, 12 inch deep pan under the manifold to catch any oil that dripped out of the manifold or cargo hoses on connection or disconnection. The lines were very heavy and had to be bolted to the manifold with 8 one inch bolts each, making the process long and tiring. If the hoses were not the same size as the manifold we had to install reducers on the manifold first. At the British supertankers, we always knew the size of the hoses, so we were always prepared. On the other end, we sometimes had problems. When the hoses came over, the ends were blanked off to prevent any spillage, and we removed the blanks over the pan. We already had the blanks off two of our manifold pipes for the connection as that was all that was necessary for the operation. When disconnecting, the shore would need to blow the hoses before we disconnected to make sure all the oil in the hoses was cleared out before attempting to disconnect, otherwise we would have more oil coming out than the pan would hold. So they would blow the hoses, then we would close the gate valves, and start unbolting the hoses. There was usually a little oil in the hoses, but not more than a few gallons. We would then blank off the hoses before allowing them to be hoisted away. The idea was to perform this operation without any oil spilling on the deck or going in the water and we were usually successful. I made a note to have the bolts, gaskets, reducers and wrenches on hand before docking.

The de-ballasting and cargo operations went well and we departed and anchored off Flamenco Island on the afternoon of the 8th for an early morning canal transit on the 9th. By 1400 we were northbound in the Caribbean once again headed for Baton Rouge. Maybe I'd get to see it after all.

I had a bit of trouble with a Japanese officer on a Japanese ship around the banks, who didn't want to yield the right of way when he was supposed to. These ships don't stop on a dime and he cut it really close. I didn't like being the stand on ship, that is the ship with the right of way, because I always had to wait to see if the other ship would do what he was supposed to; and if he didn't, I'd have to make last minute maneuvers. I preferred being the give way ship, then I could take action early enough to be safe, and leave no doubt as to my intentions for the stand on ship.

That night was a beautiful, cloudless night. The moon gave me a great horizon so I decided to take night stars. The position was just about perfect and at a good time as I was approaching Explorer Shoals. It worked out so well that I tried it again the next night in the Yucatan Channel with similar results.

The morning of the 13th the gyro pilot was out and we were on hand steering again. By noon I was taking bearings on oil rigs, headed for the Mississippi. The Mississippi was a lot narrower than I thought it would be. We slowly worked our way up on the 14th through heavy traffic. I've never seen tow boats push such huge masses of barges before. I passed two Exxon ships that were aground on that four-hour watch alone, and it was one of the noisiest watches I've ever had with the ship's pilots and tow boat captains maneuvering to avoid colliding in the current. At 1730, that evening, an evening that will live on in the memories of many, we were docking at the Exxon terminal in Baton Rouge.

Chapter 14

Baton Rouge

We took the terminal's docking master aboard, and with his assistance brought the ship in and secured it to the terminal dock. We had to put three men on the dock to handle the lines and rig the gangway because there was no dock crew. When the docking master was satisfied that we were tied up properly he signed the forms and disembarked. Things kind of went south from there.

When ship's deck crew had knocked off at 1800, and the paperwork was completed I asked the dock manager when we would start connecting the hoses, and he said that we were not tied up properly and were in an unsafe condition; we would have to re-secure the ship before he would allow connecting hoses. I questioned this, and explained that his terminal's docking master had managed and approved the docking procedure and was satisfied that the ships condition was safe. He answered me by calling the terminal manager on his radio and telling him that the whole ship's crew including the master, was drunk and that the terminal's dock crew had to tie the ship up without the help of the crew. Then I could hear them both talking on the phone with our Philadelphia office, and telling them the same thing.

Something sinister was going on here. I was on the deck at the time with the terminal's safety officer who verified that the statement the dock manager had just given to the terminal manager and the Philadelphia office was entirely false. We were all sober, and the dock crew not only did not tie up the ship, but were not even available on the dock to assist us. When I asked the dock manager what he wanted changed, he drew a pencil sketch on his pad, which was very similar to what we had been done, and told me that he had a four hour call out for dock hands, and that we would have to wait for them. As only two lines had to be moved, I sent my deck watch up to the dock to move the lines, at the strong objection of the dock manager. It only took about ten minutes. He said that we had broken union rules and that his union would go on strike and we would not be able to discharge our cargo. I replied that he, as the terminal's representative, had just told me, the ship's officer on deck, that my ship was in an unsafe condition. Under those circumstances, I, as the officer on watch, must take immediate action to secure the ship and remove it from an unsafe condition. So if he had a union problem, that was his doing, not ours. This may sound pat, but a battle can be won on the way to loosing a war, and this looked like just a skirmish.

The Exxon terminal at Baton Rouge didn't have hoses; they had chickasaw booms which were hinged pipes, hydraulically operated; a quick, easy way to make the connections. My next job was to get them connected, so we could start cargo but not only was there no boom operator on the dock, the manager wouldn't even tell me the size of the connection so we could be ready. We waited another two hours for the boom operator to show up and connect three of the booms. When connected, the terminal safety officer returned and said he had to suspend operations until all safety violations were removed and all safety requirements were met, more delays, why couldn't they have done this before?

They couldn't do it before for a very specific reason, that the safety officer told me on the sly while we were correcting safety violations. One violation was that there was no fire extinguisher by the gangway, it was only 15 feet away, but they called it a violation. Another was that there needed to be step in front of the gangway; a box that was sitting next to it sufficed. The reason for all the delays, was that the terminal was not ready for the ship; it had no room for the cargo, all of its tanks were full. If you are old enough, you will recall, that at this time in our history, the 1970s, the oil companies were claiming that there was a huge oil shortage, and the price of oil doubled.

The problem for Exxon was that it had contracted for the oil and delivery, and now had no place to put it. There is a term in shipping called demurrage. When there is a delay with a ship in port, there is an expense. The party causing the delay has to pay the injured party the costs involved. If the BC was delayed for one day, the cost would be about 20,000 dollars that Exxon would have to pay to the ship. If, on the other hand, the BC performed poorly and stayed at the dock longer than expected, the ship would have to pay Exxon for the extended use of their facility. In our case, the terminal was at fault, due to scheduling errors, but was trying to place blame on the ship, claiming it was unsafe, so it could get out of paying. This was big business and they had no problem ruining people's careers to save a few dollars. I know what happened at the terminal; they totally mismanaged the scheduling, and then tried to misdirect attention onto a fabricated ship's crew problem.

When the booms were placed and the safety requirements met, the dock manager called the surveyors to gage the ship. They were dragging this out as long as possible while they shifted oil around in shore tanks trying to get enough room. The surveyors "forgot" their thermometers, so I had to get ours for them. Then, when they pulled them out of the tanks, they failed to use rags and sprayed oil on the deck and on my clothes. Where these guys inept or were they trying to make a mess?

The captain was called ashore by the company, never to return; he had lasted only one trip. I knocked on the chief mate's door when I was ready to start cargo operations. Until then, neither Vich nor Larry had come out on deck. I think they knew there was trouble and expected the chief mate to fix it. At any rate, they were hiding, when they could have been on deck to help straighten things out. When the chief came out I could tell he had been drinking. He told me that I was in charge of the cargo operations for this port, because he was being relieved of his duties. Then he asked me what went wrong, and why this was happening. I just told him that he was in the wrong place at the wrong time. There are those who have no qualms about lying, cheating, and stealing to avoid taking responsibility for their actions. There are the others who believe these lies because they would not have the audacity to do such things themselves, and wouldn't suspect others of it. The captain and chief mate were being replaced because someone was trying to get out of something. The chief resorted to drinking and that pretty much ended it for him; now there was no way to prove that he wasn't drunk on deck. I happened to be there, on deck, demanding satisfaction, and I wasn't going to roll over and play dead. This was my first ship, and I didn't want to be fired. I went to Vich's room and he told me that if the chief mate wasn't working cargo, then he wasn't either but he would stand his watch and give me a hand if I needed him. Larry said he would be back for his watch but he was going to a hotel until this thing blew over. He suggested that I do the same.

So I went out on deck, told the pumpman to get the pumps warmed up in recirculation and get ready to start cargo. I requested that the shore valves be opened so we could start the cargo, but I really didn't care if they opened them or not. We had already been delayed over 4 hours and I wanted to establish that we were ready, and that any delays from here on could not be blamed on us. With the shore valves open, we opened out manifold valves and kicked up the pumps to discharge speed. Usually, things quieted down at this point as we were pulling out of full tanks. I checked the manifold pressures, and found them to be excessive – over 120 lbs. They were normally about 60 to 70. I called up to the dock manager and told him that we were getting excessive pressures and to check his valves.

One of the booms started to leak and I had to shut down. Then we had to wait for the dock to send someone down to check the boom. They decided that it had to be disconnected and reseated, but "forgot" to blow it out before disconnecting and dumped oil all over the manifold and deck. We had to clean up the mess before we could resume discharging. I entered a protest that the dock personnel failed to connect the chickasaw correctly and caused a spill on deck, placing the delay at their door. I wanted to make sure they knew that any delays, including those caused be excessive manifold pressures were the responsibility of the terminal. After starting again, the pressures were still excessive so I called the manager again and told him to check his valves to make sure they were completely open. He said they were, but I didn't believe him, he didn't say it with conviction. I kept the hourly manifold pressure log for documentation because I remembered in the charter agreement (remember the charter agreement that that Captain made me read?) that we had to maintain the minimum discharge rate specified unless there was excessive back pressure exceeding 110 lbs at the manifold gauges. As long as the oil was going out, and the pressure was over 110, I didn't care how slow it was, although I was concerned about the excessive pressure on the ship's deck lines.

I'd been on deck for seventeen hours when Larry came back at 0440, almost an hour late. While he was on deck I gauged off the ship and went back to the lounge to calculate the discharge rate. It was slow, less than half the normal rate. Larry called on the radio at 0750 and said he was going to breakfast then back to the hotel. I saw him in the mess hall.

"You're crazy. Working cargo is the worst job on the ship. It's the chief's job, not ours."

"Look – I'm not going to sit around and wait to be sent home. With or without your help I'm emptying this ship." I stated emphatically.

"That's ridiculous; we don't have to do anything. They won't send us home; it's not our fault. Cargo is the chief's job, shut it down; wait for a new chief." He continued. "I'll show up and stand my watch, but I'm not working cargo."

"You do what you think you should, but unless the company tells me otherwise, I'm drying this ship out and getting it ready for sea."

"You're nuts." He said as he got up from the table and headed to the door.

On deck I checked the manifold pressure and asked the dock manager why they were holding us back and he said they were keeping us at a low rate because they were topping off tanks.

Well, that pretty much said it all. I logged that time and statement for future reference.

I was stripping out the wing tanks when Larry came back. About that time the dock manager told me that he was going to shut us down if I didn't find out who borrowed someone's bicycle on the dock – really!

A guy from the ship chandler arrived on the dock.

"Permission for the chandler to come aboard Captain?" he requested.

"I'm not the captain." I responded while I was writing down the gauge pressures.

"Is the captain aboard?"

"No, He's been relieved of duty." I stated while I moved along the manifold bridge.

"Well, is the chief mate aboard then?"

"No, He's been relieved as well."

"Second mate?"

"Off, in town."

"Who's in charge?"

"Just me, I'm the third"

"Well, if you're the only licensed officer aboard, and you're in charge, then believe it or not, you're the captain. Permission to come aboard Captain?"

"Come aboard." It was a simple logic, although I don't think it really worked that way. I looked over his papers and signed them.

"Everything should be here by 0100."

I thought here meant right here. I didn't know it meant a mile away at the terminal gate.

I finished cargo just before midnight and then waited for 90 minutes for the surveyors to show up and another hour for someone to disconnect the cargo booms. The terminal would not clear us to take ballast until all covers were on the manifold with bolts in every hole, and we didn't even use deck lines for ballast. When our truckload of stores arrived at the terminal, we had to send the crew to hand-carry them from the gate over a mile away - talk about inhospitable.

While waiting for a new captain and chief mate, our union officials came aboard to get a statement from me as to the condition of the captain the previous night. It wasn't much of a statement for there wasn't anything wrong with the captain. Then the SOHIO port captain visited us and spoke to us as though we had the academic capacity of third graders. I hope he was acting, because if he wasn't, SOHIO was in trouble too. When our new captain arrived, he was in a sour mood and yelled at me on his way through to his new office. It didn't bother me as I was too busy trying to complete the cargo papers as best as I could, and figured he was just another guy that didn't get much warning. The ship's appearance probably had something to do with it as well.

The docking master arrived after I had turned in all the paperwork and I took him up to the bridge. We were waiting for Exxon to decide if we needed one tug or two for departure before letting go. They finally decided on one and it came alongside. But as we were letting the lines go they changed their mind and told us to wait for a second tug. There were no others left because they were all downstream trying to free the *EXXON BALTIMORE* that had grounded. We secured another tug that was coming down river, but by the time we had her, the first one left to take a pilot somewhere. When that one came back a half hour later, we cleared the dock and started down river.

We passed the EXXON *BALTIMORE* a few miles down on the west side, hard up. If I never go back to Baton Rouge, I was there one too many times. I'd been up for two days, but had succeeded in running my first cargo operation without a major mishap (excluding loosing the captain and chief mate). We were now on our way, south bound in the Mississippi without a chief mate. I was sent to the bow to stand by the anchor while we transited a particular section of the river and finally retired for some rest; I'd had 2 hours off in the last 56 hours and was in for 3 solid hours of sleep before the morning watch. I was beyond exhausted, there was a buzzing in my head, my vision was fuzzy, and sounds seemed very sharp with a tin echo. I slowly climbed the ladder to the tween deck and shuffled to the next ladder, it was just thirty more feet to my room. I pulled my way up and entered the passageway, just ten more feet. I fumbled with the knob, tripped over the threshold and fell in a heap, face down on my rack. My eyes closed and wouldn't open, the buzzing continued. My arms wouldn't move; I let go.

> Oh sleep! It is a gentle thing,
> Beloved from pole to pole!
> To Mary Queen the praise be given!
> She sent the gentle sleep from Heaven,
> That slid into my sole.
> THE RIME OF THE ANCIENT MARINER
> Samuel Taylor Coleridge

At twenty-two years old, with three months time in, I felt like an ancient mariner.

Chapter 15

A New Crew

I forced myself to the bridge for the midnight watch; pulling myself along the passageways and dragging my legs, first one, then the other until I got up to the chartroom. My three-hour nap hadn't helped; I was drowsy and light headed. I seemed to be in slow motion and didn't understand anything I read in the night order book or the ship's log. I looked at the chart. Vich saw me and came into the chartroom.

"Are you all right?" he asked with that course voice.

"Yeah, I'm good." I replied, blinking and squinting to try to see where we were on the chart.

"Right here." He stated, tapping his forefinger on the chart at a location on the river with some pencil marks.

"Okay, I got it." I said as I placed the dividers on the chart pointing at the location. My hands were shaking.

"We're on hand steering and full ahead, maneuvering speed. The pilot is on the bridge, and the captain just went below for a few minutes." Then he ducked down the ladder, and I went into the pantry and poured a fresh cup of coffee. I didn't usually use sugar in my coffee but that morning I used three teaspoons. I knew I wouldn't like the taste but I needed a kick-start badly. My hands didn't stop shaking for another ten minutes. I walked into the dark wheelhouse.

"Good morning Mr. Pilot." I greeted the pilot with a mostly stable voice.

"Good morning sir, and how are you this morning?" He responded.

"Tired sir, what are we steering?"

"Your helmsman is lined up on the range up ahead. We'll change as we pass that northbound tow. I looked ahead and saw the range lights on shore just before the next bend in the river."

"Very good sir" I commented as I looked at the heading, and the range lights. Then, noting the time I went into the chart room to get a better look at the chart. My head was starting to clear. I marked off the four miles we traveled since Vich left, and searched on the chart for something to take a bearing on. I went out to the bridge wing and looked at the buoy lights, noting the approximate position in the river and then went back into the chart room to see if I could see any of the buoys that I had spotted in the river. I had a winner. I made a few trips back and forth until I was very familiar with the section of river we were on, and then settled in for the morning.

"Let's put her Half Ahead Mr. Mate." suggested the pilot. I say he suggested it because the pilot is only an adviser on the ship. The responsibility for safe navigation always rests with the ship's officer. But even though the pilot only suggests an operation it is understood as a command in most cases; the exception being when the officer believes the suggestion would put the ship in danger or lacks the prudence with which the ship is normally operated.

"Half Ahead." I repeated and moved the engine order telegraph pointer to "HALF AHEAD". The EOT bell started ringing, and stopped when the engineer matched my setting down below. Then I went over to the RPM indicator and waited a few seconds for the revolutions to decrease to 36. "We're at half ahead sir." I added when the engineers got the rpms down to 36. I made the entry in the Bell Book.

"Thank you." The pilot returned.

"Ten degrees right rudder." The pilot requested.

"Ten degrees right rudder." returned the helmsman as he turned the wheel to get ten degrees on the rudder "The rudder is right ten degrees" added the helmsman when the rudder was in the appropriate position. The ship started to swing to starboard with increasing speed.

"Ease to 5" the pilot requested.

"Easing to 5" returned the helmsman, adding "She's at 5" a few moments later.

"Mid-ships" the pilot suggested.

"Mid-ships" returned the helmsman, as he brought the rudder back to center.

"Can you see the range lights coming into line ahead?" asked the pilot, pointing to two lights on land that were lining up as the ship rounded the bend in the river.

"Yes sir." answered the helmsman.

"Steer on that range. We want to keep her on that range. "

"Yes sir."

The sides of the ship are port (left) and starboard (right), but on American ships, the steering commands are given as left or right, not port or starboard. This is an American tradition, not followed on foreign ships, and it causes confusion with foreign pilots who only revert to left and right on American ships. To aid the helmsman further, there is a placard posted on the forward bulkhead of the bridge in front of the steering console with the words "LEFT" and "RIGHT" with arrows to show which direction each is. Although that may seem absurd, you must remember that even at that time there were some sailors that couldn't read (so what was the point of the words?), some sailors that were foreign (with the proper work permits), and some sailors that simply couldn't remember which way was which. Of course, American pilots were used to this, unless they worked in the Panama Canal.

Transiting the Mississippi was a tedious business. I wasn't used to that much noise and confusion. There were these tow boats each towing 12-20 barges, and the ships that were aground at various places. Then there were all those lights. The river was a ribbon of black winding through the towns and cities that merged into one giant urban park. As we approached New Orleans the lights got brighter and the radio noise increased. I doubt I could have gotten down that river without the pilot on a ship the size of the BC. Larry was late to the bridge again – Late Larry.

I awoke to the hellacious noise of pounding and scraping outside my room at 0900. (Please keep in mind, I lived in a steel box.) I had counted on more than five hours of sleep that morning. I opened the blackout to the view of the crew chipping and scraping paint outside my room. There hadn't been any deck work on the ship since I joined back in July. Did it have to start that day? I couldn't get back to sleep or even think straight with all that noise. The lounge wasn't any better; it was next to my room.

I went down to the mess deck to see if there was anything to eat, circumspectly avoiding the grape nuts. I had some cereal and went aft to see the delta area. I had finished reading "Human Destiny", a very good book but a bit heavy, and was about half way through "The Burnished Blade" a much lighter and more entertaining book. I didn't have the concentration to read on deck, I found myself too drawn to the water and lost in thought. I went in for lunch. By noon we had taken departure and were back at sea. The pilot boat that retrieved the pilot also delivered a new chief mate; I hadn't met him yet, but his license was posted. I took care of the noon business and was maneuvering through the oil rigs when the captain came up to the bridge.

Captain Daniels was a tall man, about 6'2", and had a trim build. He was forty-five or fifty years old, had dark, short wavy hair and was dressed completely in denim; pants, shirt and vest. He started, "Where did you get those pants?" I didn't know what he meant until he said they practically blinded him when he came on the bridge. I looked down. I was wearing a pair of bright red and yellow plaid pants. Now, its not that I like outlandish clothes, or that my taste of style is much different than anyone else; its just that I don't like to waste things and when someone gave me something that I would be embarrassed to wear, I stuck it in my bottom drawer. All the clothes that went into that drawer ended up in my sea bag. I didn't think any one out here would care; apparently I was wrong. They were a good pair of pants, wore like iron, just a little abrasive on the eyes.

He continued. "I want to apologize for yelling at you when I first came on. I was pretty upset at being called out on such short notice, and everyone was in an uproar about what happened on the ship. Yet, you seem to be the only one who did anything. As a matter of fact, it looks like you took care of everything, and with all that, I was yelling at you. I'm really am sorry about that."

"Well Captain, it was a tough port. But the problem was not with the ship; it was with the terminal. The captain was not drunk, nor even on deck, and the ship was secured safely, the chief mate saw to that, and he wasn't drunk either; no one had been drinking. I can't believe they took the wild accusation of a terminal dock manager over their own docking master and safety officer. I can't believe they fired them."

"Yet" he continued, "You took on the chief mate's job and emptied out the ship. When I got here, I expected to be in port for a few days, waiting for a new chief and then for him to empty out the ship before we could leave. You had the ship ready for sea; you even ballasted it."

"And I would have left if I'd gotten the orders to." I interjected, as a joke.

He was quiet for a few seconds, and then added "I don't think that's as much of a joke as you think; I think you really would have taken this ship down river if they told you to."

"Well, maybe."

"Well. You have a few days to finish the job."

"Finish? What's left?" I asked.

"All the paperwork for the port, and you're the only one that can do it. You're the only one who knows what happened.

"Oh –. " I thought I had completed everything. When I went below after watch, I couldn't believe the amount of paperwork that had yet to be done. I guess that's why the chief mate was a full time day worker. Our new chief mate, Mark

Mathews, was an average size man, about 5'9", a little stocky but not fat, with short black hair and a short beard, fortyish, and had a quiet presence about him that suggested more toward slyness than shyness. I found him in his new office behind a mountain of paperwork that I had the unpleasant task of reducing by half.

"Uh, Chief?"

"Yeah, what can I...Oh, hey, you're the third?"

"Well, I'm one of the thirds."

"Yeah, but you're THE third, the one who ran the operations, right?"

"Yeah, that would be me."

"Hey, uh, we have to talk about the plumbing; I can't find the diagrams... And who's been..uh, wait..you emptied out the ship; do you think you can load it?"

"Sure, no problem, I can walk you through it."

"Did you ever try these?" He asked, holding out a big cigar to me.

"No, never smoked a cigar." I replied.

"You gotta try one of these, they're Nicaraguan, as good as Cuban. Here, take one, if you like it I can get you some."

"No thanks, I don't smoke, it would just be wasted."

"Suit yourself."

We separated my part of the paper and the mountain came to me.

Captain Daniels did not like the look of the ship, I guess he agree with the rest of us. And he had no problem putting the crew to work to get things cleaned up. The crew took on a new look as they were finally able to work and make some money instead of lying about looking depressed day after day. I negotiated for the crew to work somewhere other than outside my room in the morning hours when I normally slept.

I worked on the cargo forms every afternoon, after watch from 1600 to 2000, excepting dinner and dinner relief for the next few days. I had to figure out how to fill in the cargo reports and logs and I had very little confidence that I had them correct. And I will admit that there were some times and numbers that I estimated because I hadn't taken note of them during the operations. When they were as complete as I could get them, I handed them in to be reviewed. I still had the port log (one of my normal jobs), and the Panama canal paperwork to do before we got to Panama. (And let's not forget the safety inspections.)

The fire and boat drill on the afternoon of the 17th went as expected in the southern gulf. On the morning of the 18th the captain came up to the bridge at 0100, very unusual in this business, unless the ship was approaching port.

"Good morning." he said as he stepped into the wheelhouse.

"Good morning." I responded a little surprised. "We're steady on 153, Captain, south of the oil fields." I added for his efficacy; I had no idea why he would be on the bridge in the middle of the Gulf of Mexico at one in the morning. He slowly walked over to the captain's chair and sat down. I looked back into the chart room; in twenty minutes my friend could be by. I wondered if Captain Daniels would pick up on him. So far, no one else had, or at least no one admitted it.

"I have another apology to make." He started. "Yesterday I came up to the bridge and started to make fun of your clothes, and that was wrong of me. I'm not saying those pants didn't warrant it, but there was no need for me to do that."

"That's okay Captain, I know they're a little loud. I wear them here because I can't wear them ashore."

"Yes, but I, of all people, should have nothing to say about clothes. You see, all I wear is denim, jeans, dungarees. I have denim pants, shirts vests, jackets, coats and even all my suits are denim. I haven't worn anything but denim for over fifteen years. And I was making fun of you for wearing normal clothes. The next port we get to, I'm going to buy some normal clothes."

"Well, Captain, if it's Freeport, I know a very good place."

"There's another thing." He added. "When you type out the crew list for Panama, I need you to change my name a little."

"How's that Captain?"

"I need you to put my name in as Baniels or Maniels or something like that."

"Why's that?" I asked.

"They're kind of looking for me down there. I was a Canal Pilot, and there was some trouble about one of the native girls."

"Okay Captain, but won't they check your license?"

"No, depending on who we get, we'll be okay."

"Well Captain, I'm not the best typist and I'm sure there will be a few typos on that list. You can see if it's good enough a day out."

"Thanks. I'll see you in the morning." He went below.

That was some line. I wondered if he really had been a canal pilot. I wondered what he was really hiding from. Why did he get on a ship going to Panama if he was wanted down there? I doubted his story; another nut case. That was the only time the captain showed up on the bridge in open water in the early morning hours.

I went into the chartroom and put a 0120 position on the chart. John didn't show; I wondered if he was gone for good.

Chapter 16

Back to Panama

We passed the Cape San Antonio light to port on the morning of the 19th. Larry was still showing up ten to fifteen minutes late for watch every day, and I was arriving for dinner as they were closing down, because he was late getting back to the bridge. By noon we were around the Misteriosa Bank navigating with sun lines. After watch I had to start on the Canal papers - the crew list, cargo manifest, and stores requisition. The stores requisition was long for this trip, it looked like the flood gates opened and everyone who wanted anything got heard. It looked like Daniels planned on staying, and he wasn't planning to live on a garbage scow.

On the midnight watch I sighted the wreck on Gorda bank with the radar. John was back; I had mixed feelings about that, I wonder if he knew. After watch, I finished "The Moroccan"; it was okay but not great. I picked up "The God Seeker", another Sinclair Lewis story. The last one of his was good, so this one was a good bet. I didn't know how much time I would have to read. I'd been working eighteen hours a day since Baton Rouge. I was up early on the 20th to get the Canal paperwork completed so the Captain could review it. I posted it on his door at 1100 and went down on deck for a few minutes before lunch.

The deck around the house was covered in paint chips, and the house looked like it had cancer with all the brown lead primer spotting it. Off the starboard bow I saw a familiar sight. I knew this area; we were approaching Quito Sueno, with its four freighters high and dry, looking like they were steaming along together. I made the turn after lunch on the noon watch, with the crew chipping, scraping and priming the bridge deck inside and out. That was a noisy, crowded, dirty watch. The compass binnacle top was missing so the steering compass was covered with a rag to protect it from the paint and dust. Larry had taken the top below to clean, and paint it. The binnacle itself was wood, and they stripped the old layers of varnish off it. I guess it had to get worse before it could get better.

The morning of the 21st was another great morning for midnight stars. The sky was clear and cloudless, the moon high and bright, very little motion, and no traffic. I had plotted another ideal position taken under better than ideal circumstances, showing that we were only eight hours out of Cristobal. By noon we were anchored inside the breakwaters, expecting to enter the canal around 1700 the next day. I watched other ships come into the anchor basin and listened to them anchor. It was another hot sunny day and I stayed inside mostly. I had taken the port log work sheet to the bridge to get it out of the way on watch. I finished up the canal paperwork with the Captain's corrections, after watch in the evening. The morning watch was pleasant. With the sun down, and the sea breeze, the ship cooled down. I spent most of the watch on the wings watching the ships anchored around us, and the launches taking the crews ashore. The city noises and music carried well across the harbor, and I wondered if I would ever get ashore there.

At noon we were still waiting to go. It was another hot watch so I stayed inside most of the time reading. The Pilot came aboard on dinner relief. I was waiting for him on the bridge with the captain.

"Hey, Hank, How ya doin?"

"Great Charlie." Captain Daniels answered as they shook hands.

"Is this your ship? I didn't see your name come up. Hey, you been gone a while – they're lookin for you ya know."

"Yeah, I know, I've been laying low, never thought I find myself back here so soon."

"So what's the story with that girl?"

"She was our maid, and a damn good one to. Charlie, you know you don't fool around with a good maid; they're too hard to find. That was a set up."

"Well, mums the word, but you know everyone's going to find out you're here. Too many people will see you."

"Let's hope the wrong ones don't find out."

"Good name." The pilot commented, and then added, "I never would have known."

Captain Daniels looked at me. I shrugged. "Fat fingers" I commented in a very low voice.

"Well Hank, Would you like the honors?"

"No, but thanks anyway. I'd rather my voice wasn't broadcast down here.

"Well, then, let's put her Slow Ahead."

"Slow Ahead" I called and moved the EOT handle from STOP to SLOW AHEAD. The bell rang until the engineer matched my setting. "She's turning slow ahead" I called out when the RPM indicator showed the correct RPMS. I guess he really was a Panama Canal Pilot.

I was called out to the stern for lines that evening, and was relieved by Vich at midnight. I don't know where Larry was, but he was also late to the bridge in the morning again. He must have thought our schedule was just a suggestion.

We met up with the *RESOLUTION* on the morning of the 23rd and de-ballasted to her by dinnertime. I helped the chief through his first loading on the BC and gave him sketches of the piping. I think Larry was a little ticked off that I was helping the chief mate, but someone had to, and Larry didn't like working cargo. When an officer joins a ship without a coordinated transfer of duties and information, his ramp up time will be extended due to the lack of knowledge, and the entire operation can be put at

Baltimore Canon Alongside the British Renown

Parita Bay

risk by a failure to manage that transition. General business works like that too. Our present captain and chief mate had not even met the men they replaced, who were both dismissed at the same time, under questionable circumstances. Add to that, the fact that our present second mate disliked cargo operations and avoided any part in them. That left the third mates to make the transition possible, and Vich didn't seem to like anything or anyone. Fortunately, I had learned enough about the ships piping and pumps to carry out the operations and could assist in the transition. I had no desire to be part of a disaster, nor to look incompetent, so I did what I could to make the transition as smooth as possible.

On the 24th we completed cargo operations and went north to anchor off Balboa where we stayed for a day and a half. I had noticed something was odd about the chief mate; he always seemed to be up at night, all night. We were loaded, and anchored, but he always seemed to have work to last through the night. At first I thought he was trying to get to know the ship, but then he was setting up the gear for tank cleaning, now it was fixing or testing some valves. Another odd thing was that I didn't usually see him in the day time. He was a day worker, 8-5, but his door was always closed during the day. Anyway, we went through the canal on the 26th. Captain Daniels had gotten through twice without the authorities knowing.

I called the captain up to the bridge before I sent down the noon report to see what he wanted to do about the mileage. He told me that we were where we were and that was all there was to it, and to log it as it was. That sounded good to me, but I wondered how long it would last. The bridge was painted inside and out that day, and we had the weekly fire and boat drill. The bridge deck was painted in parts over the next few days so we could still work. There was a dramatic improvement in my working environment; it still didn't look good, but it looked a lot better. Larry brought up the compass binnacle cover; it was a highly polished brass. He had taken all those layers of paint off and polished it. It was the sharpest looking thing on the bridge.

That night and the next morning we traveled through a fishing fleet. We were off the Gorda Bank, which looked like a good area to fish, but I don't recall seeing any fishing boats in this area before. On the bank the water is mostly between thirty and sixty feet deep except in a few areas on the northwest end where there is a small island and some rocks. These are mostly made up debris that was blown in or washed up in storms, including the wreck that we used as a radar contact that was stuck on Farrell Rocks. We were headed back to Calcaseau Pass and Lake Charles.

A new third A/E had joined in Baton Rouge as well. He was an older guy, maybe sixtyish, and he was small and thin. He was an amateur painter and had brought his supplies with him. I think he was a late comer to the business because the chief engineer was always making comments about him devoting more time to engineering and less to painting. He seemed more inclined to leisure than overtime and that didn't wash in the engine department. The chief engineer wanted all of his officers on overtime every day whether he needed them or not. I was all over that engine room every week to inspect the fire stations and change out fire extinguishers - it was hot, noisy, dirty, and smelly. I wouldn't want to be there sixteen hours a day either.

Bob (the new Third A/E) wanted to go ashore in Lake Charles to get more canvas and he invited me along. I agreed to go with him, because I'd have someone to split the cab fare with, and I'd probably get into less trouble with Bob than on my own. But that was a few days off; we weren't even up to my new shallow spot yet. We had the only chart in the world that showed that shallow. The 29th was a day of rain and squalls in the lower gulf but the LORAN was working so we were good for navigation. The captain came up at noon, and looked over the chart. He had a slip of paper in his hand that he placed on the chart table, and told me we were going to have to do something about the mileage. I read the note; it was a wire from the company. He was being warned by the company the same way I had been warned by the first captain. Captain Daniels didn't want to be fired either. The squalls quickly brought the weather to Force 6.

We entered the fairway at the junction below Calcasieu Pass and proceeded northwest toward the pass on the morning of the 31st with the weather rapidly subsiding.

We were alongside by 1600 and the captain paid off the crew and closed articles at 1800. I don't know why he did that unless it had something to do with the Baton Rouge problem. They were 12-month articles and we were only a few months into them. I was given the option of leaving, as both, the articles were closed, and I had been aboard just about four months. Most officers left after four months, but I had decided from the beginning to stay six, and I wanted to stick to that plan. So I stayed - I went ashore for the night, but I stayed signed on. Larry, on the other hand, signed off and went home, and we got another new second mate, the fourth since I arrived.

When filling out my overtime sheet for the month of October, I added thirty-one hours for restriction to ship in Panama. We were supposed to get launch service but never did, and I wanted to see the town. Larry said that we could claim overtime for restriction to ship if we were anchored in a safe port for more than twelve hours and the captain didn't provide launch service. So that's what I did. The captain wasn't pleased, and disputed it. So we sent the paper work in and waited. Even without the disputed overtime, I had logged over 200 hours of overtime for that month.

We had a hard time finding art supplies for Bob (who wore a suit to town), and eventually gave up. So we went out for a good dinner and Bob insisted on paying. I had a good time, didn't drink too much, and made it back on time, and in shape for watch. When I took the deck watch at midnight I heard that our union representative had been aboard and was looking for me. Usually they just want to collect the dues, and as far as I knew, I was paid up. He may have wanted to discuss the disputed overtime, but our union wasn't really interested in disputes so I doubt it. Anyway, I didn't ever hear from him after that, so it couldn't have been that important.

The new second mate relieved me at 0400 on deck. I stayed around for an hour so I could get him situated and familiar with the ship, then ducked out before the chief could tell me he wanted me to stay on deck. I probably should have stayed, because when I came out at noon, I had to re-strip all the tanks before they would certify us dry. After the gauging, we were allowed to open the sea chest valves and start ballasting. I set the sailing board for 2200, to shift over to an anchorage to take bunkers and turned the deck over to the new second.

I was on the stern at 2200 for undocking and when I returned to my room, at 2330, I found myself locked out. I couldn't get the key to work. I went up to the bridge to take the midnight watch and notified the chief mate about the lock. It took them (the captain, chief mate, third mate and third A/E) two hours to get the door opened, and the lock was totally destroyed. So from then on, I was unable to lock my room in port.

In the afternoon we picked up the anchor, and headed south toward the gulf. I took the morning watch in the fairway, a section marked on the chart for safe navigation through the oil rigs. Later in the morning I worked on the cargo ullage report and tanker discharge record. I don't think I was supposed to be filling these in, but the chief gave them to me to do.

The morning of November 4th, we were off the Bank of Campeche headed for the eastern Yucatan Channel when I turned over the watch in light weather, with a slight roll and our usual vibration caused by our light condition. I woke later that morning at 1000 to the sound of rushing water. As I swung my legs around the rail at the side of my rack, I put my feet down in two inches of water. There was two inches of water in my room, shifting with the roll, and my shoes were floating in it. I knew it; we were finally sinking. I jumped on the rack and opened up the black out expecting to see water up to the officer's deck. But we were riding high, and still vibrating - so where was this water from. I stepped back into the water and grabbed my shoes, then opened the door. The passage way was dry. The thresh hold from my door kept the water in. I got my dry shoes from the drawer and carried them out. I put them on in the passageway and walked down the hall to the water closet for a mop and bucket. I returned and mopped out the room, and my locker. I couldn't seem to get the locker dry, the water seemed to keep filling back up. I got cleaned up for watch and by the time I got out of the shower, the floor was wet again. I put my shoes on the dresser to dry, and carried my dry ones and my socks out to the passageway with a towel. I put them on out there and put the towel on the dresser top just inside the door. Then I closed the door and went down for lunch. At lunch I told the chief engineer about the problem and he said I must have left the water running (like I wouldn't notice that!). I told him that I dried out the room and thirty minutes later it was wet again, and there was no water running. He said that I must have shut the water off and not to worry, it will dry up by itself. I went up to the bridge. We passed Cuba and headed south to the banks in the Caribbean. At 1400 the BR (from the steward's staff) came up to the bridge and told me that my room was flooded, but not to worry, he mopped it out dry. Our new second mate came up to the bridge on time and I went below to see if I should put on my swimming trunks – I wouldn't have looked out of place. I stopped in the chief mate's office to ask for some negotiating help. He said he'd look into it. At dinner, I asked the 1st A/E to look into the water in my room. He said the deck hands must have been washing something down outside my room, it would probably dry up on its own.

After dinner relief I took a nap for a few hours leaving my shoes and socks on the dresser top. I got up at the 2315 call to the sound of rushing water. I got up and wandered around in it, getting what I needed and getting to the bathroom, then stepped out into the passageway, grabbed the shoes, socks and towel off the dresser, put the shoes and socks on and stowed the towel on the dresser before closing the door. The next day we were off the banks steaming through fishing boats again, and I was still wading around in my room. The 7th brought no relief from the flooding. I found that as long as I kept up with the mopping (about every hour), I could be fairly dry.

We anchored in the inner anchorage in Cristobal on the afternoon of the 7th, and at 1800 I went ashore in Panama for the first time.

Chapter 17

Finally Ashore in Panama

I headed out on deck after dinner to catch the first launch ashore, scheduled for 1800. Kevin, the new second mate, was already at the pilot ladder waiting for me. I let Vich know that I was going, and would return on the midnight launch, in case the launch was late for some reason. I took my turn with half the ship's crew, climbing down the pilot ladder to the boat. When the last man was aboard we pushed off and motored into the dock, about a twenty-minute ride. The boat dock was crowded and noisy with launches coming and going. The world's sailors met here every day for a few hours ashore while the ships waited for their convoys. We fell into the stream of men working their way along the wharf toward the gate that divided the city into its halves. Cristobal, the American side controlled by the Panama Canal governance was fenced off from Colon, on the Panamanian side. We waved our "Z" cards as we passed the guard at the gate and entered Panama. On the Panamanian side of the fence, off to the right were a gang of boys and young men shouting and waving to us. These were "shore pilots" looking for an engagement for the evening. We weren't interested at that time, but these guys are a great help if you are looking for something specific and don't want to waste time.

The mass of sailors swarmed onto Thirteenth Street, a rather dirty thoroughfare, and started to diffuse at Bolivar Avenue. By the time we reached Guerrero Avenue (the second street after

Bolivar) and were ready to get off the main drag, Kevin pulled out a reefer and lit it up.

"Hey, put that thing out." I warned him. "These cops have machine guns." And indeed, we had already passed several police officers, dressed in fatigues, carrying machine guns.

"Ah, they won't bother us. Here, try this."

"No thanks. I don't smoke that crap; I don't smoke anything. I don't want to be any where near that stuff around here." I stated emphatically.

"Ah, I thought we would do some partying tonight." Kevin half complained.

"We will, but not with that stuff."

He put the reefer out and stuck it in his shirt pocket for a later time and we squeezed into a small restaurant to check out the local cuisine. I found a small table near the back and we sat down. It was so noisy and crowded that we couldn't hear each other. The place was filthy, it had low ceilings and the stench was overpowering. I signaled to Kevin to follow me out. I wasn't going to eat in a dump like that. We walked down one of the side streets toward a place that was giving off the sounds of a good time. When we got to the door I heard shouts from within, and a few seconds later Robel and Menendez came out.

"Hey, Mate..C'mon in; have a drink with us." The rest were coming toward the door, hooting and hollering. It looked like half of our crew was crammed into that place and they were making room for two more. Kevin wasn't too sure about this, he hadn't been with the crew for long, but I was good. Anyway we chatted for a few minutes at the door and I made our excuses about being expected somewhere, and made them understand that we would be happy to stay another time, or even later that night. Then we moved along down the street to find a quieter, less crowded firetrap. We found just such a place a few streets over, on the other side of Thirteenth Street.

From the street, it was like walking into a cave. The bar was a good thirty feet back from the door and I had to let my eyes adjust to the darkness. The place was also dimly lit, with low music and some type of fabric hanging from the ceiling. There were only about ten customers or so it seemed at that moment. The bar stools were all taken, but there were empty chairs scattered about. They were very low to the floor, almost like beach chairs, and the tables were low as well. I went over to the bar and tried for Negro Modelo but had to settle for San Miguel. It was probably better for us any way. San Miguel was made with quinine water; it tasted worse, but was healthier for the environment. I handed one to Kevin and we wandered over to the low chairs, and sat down with our cheap beer. That's about the time I realized that there were only about five other customers. The other five were girls, working girls. Two of them came over to our short table, and it seems they were trying to sell their wares. I looked at Kevin. "Are we where I think we are?" I asked.

"It appears so." He replied.

"Well, I don't want to get mixed up in this." I said. Then to the girls, "Estamos aqui para cerveza solamente.", which I believe means something like "We're only here for the beer." I hoped they weren't insulted, and we didn't get booted out. They went back over to the bar, probably figuring we didn't speak their language well enough to have a meaningful conversation. We didn't.

We got another round a short while later and were resting comfortably until I thought I saw something shoot across the floor in the shadows.

"What was that?"

"Probably a rat" Kevin explained.

"They got rats here?"

"Everybody has rats down here, why do you think they keep it so dark? Don't worry, they won't bother you; there's enough garbage lying around to keep them busy."

Another one of the girls came over and attempted to communicate with us using the only two words of English that she knew, and pointed up and over to the stairs.

"No, no, no" I said, shaking my head and waving her away.

She looked at Kevin and pointed to the stairs. Kevin got up. "Actually, I think I'll go with her, watch my beer. You don't mind, do you?"

"No, go ahead."

Off they went and I sat there for a while, until a stool opened up. I got up, grabbed the stool, and put our beer on the bar and got my feet off the floor, away from the vermin. I had a third beer while I waited. Kevin eventually came back looking none the worse for wear.

"Don't tell anyone on the ship about this."

"I won't, it's your business, no one else's."

"Thanks"

It was odd, Kevin didn't want to have a drink with his ship mates because he didn't know them that well, but thought nothing about being familiar with a girl he'd never seen before, in a house of ill repute (or maybe just a house of plain repute in this town), going upstairs for what ever could be waiting for him. And as for the not telling any one, by the time we reached state side, he'd told every one on the ship himself.

We finished our beer and wandered out and back to the place the rest of the crew had been at, but they had gone off in search of greener pastures. So we headed back to the dock, and hung around there waiting for the 2330 launch. The 12-4 watch straggled in a few minutes before the scheduled departure, and were on board in time for watch. The 8-12 crew was waiting on deck and descended to the launch when we all arrived topside. They would probably be out all night, returning for their watch at 0800. Robel, my Ordinary, spent all of his money ashore, 1200 dollars! That's two hundred dollars an hour! Apparently he was just giving his money away; I guess he liked to. I don't think I spent more than twenty bucks.

We weighed anchor at 1300 on the 8th, went through the canal, and continued on to the *RENOWN* for immediate berthing

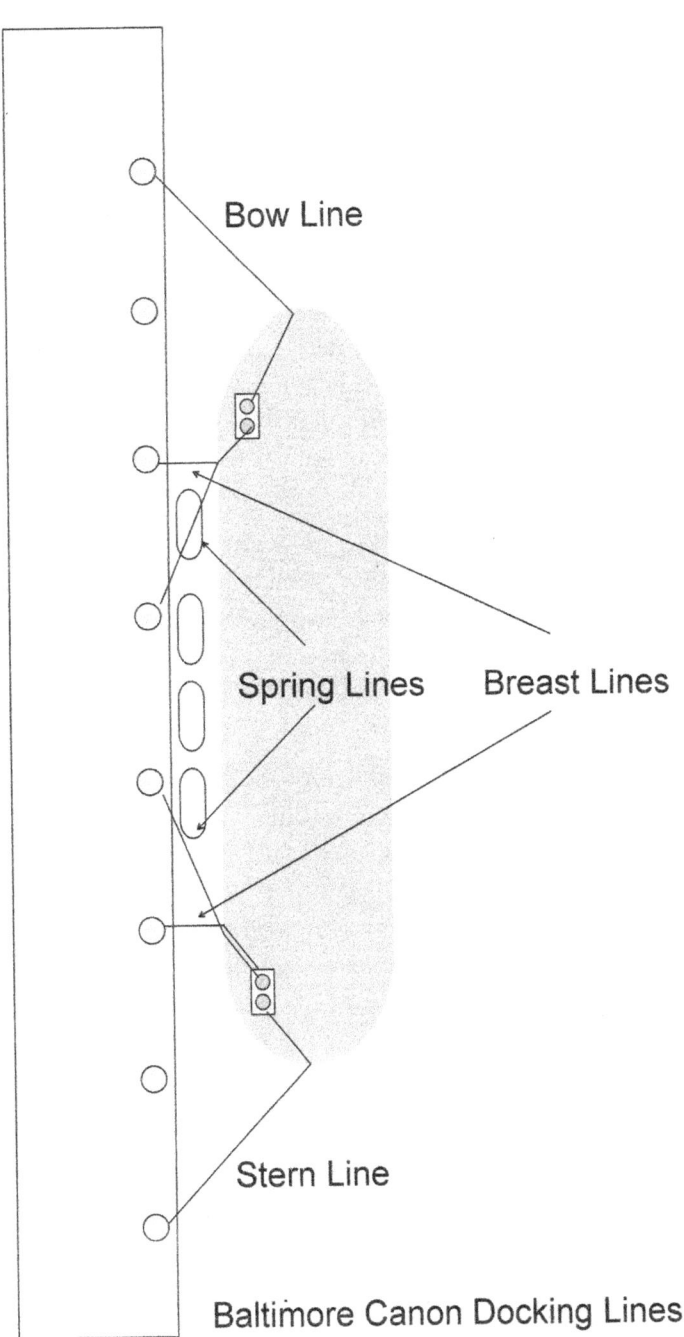

Baltimore Canon Docking Lines

at 0030. I had the deck for the berthing. Usually, the third mate is on the bridge for docking, but I seemed to be working lines quite a bit this last month. I don't think Kevin liked the crew. And as it turned out, I had a little tiff on deck while tying up to the RENOWN. One of the new ABs, Sunnto, a black guy, maybe about 6'4", weighed in at about 250 pounds (all muscle), was bald and had one of the nastiest dispositions I'd ever seen. I'd watched him work lines on the stern in the locks. When he took up a line, the rest of the crew all stepped back. He threw mooring lines around like they were heaving lines, and the cursing and other foul language that came from that guy was enough to make the sailors take cover. Kevin and Vich just left him alone to do as he wanted, but I had lines on this morning, and I didn't like to leave a mess.

The first line out from the stern was the spring line (as per the docking master's orders). The Preacher sent the heaving line over and the crew on the RENOWN pulled in our spring line and put the eye over a bitt. We tightened it up and secured it on our end, and then Sunnto started flinging the extra line on deck in a heap. Every one else stepped back while this mad man made a rats nest of the line.

"Hey, you're doing that wrong." I yelled out, stepping toward him. In the dead silence on the afterdeck I had a few moments to think about what I had just started. As he strode over to me, I was thinking, what's the worse he can do? He can hit me, but if he does, he'll loose his papers and never sail again. A sailor can't hit an officer without loosing his papers and going to jail. (I failed to follow that thought through though; if he hit me, he'd probably have killed me.) He stood over me, glowering down at me; I could see the crew moving back a little further. No one wanted to be any where near this.

"Mate" he said with his hands clenched, "I've been doing it this way for twenty years"

Looking up, and without letting him finish, I jumped in with "Then you've been doing it wrong for twenty years. You'll do it my way." We stared at each other for a few seconds, then he threw his hands in the air.

"Well...alright then, but I won't be responsible..."

"You're not responsible, I am. So do it my way."

Sunnto strode back to the line, stretched it out on deck, and without any instruction, started faking the line out properly. The line has to be faked out properly so it can run free if necessary, without tangling. Sunnto knew this, and he knew how to do it properly. I grew about four inches taller that day, about the same amount that Sunnto shrunk. I never had any more trouble from Sunnto, or the rest of the crew while I was on that ship, and all the ship's lines were laid out properly from that day on.

I started de-ballasting before turning over the watch to Kevin, but when I came back eight hours later we were still pumping out the ballast. I don't know what happened but eleven hours was way to long for de-ballasting. Once again I was re-stripping the tanks with the deep well pump to get the dry certificate. Kevin took over as I was checking tanks with the Caleb Brett surveyors. At some point Mark (the chief mate) was going to have to figure out how to strip the tanks dry; I didn't think the company was going to stand for those delays for long. I wondered if they even noticed.

I topped off the wing tanks on the morning of the 10th leaving the center tanks for the chief and second mate. The chief had me called out in the morning to fill out the departure papers and I think he got yelled at by the captain because the chief was supposed to do the cargo and departure papers. So I had breakfast and went back for some sleep.

By noon we were anchored at Balboa. Kevin went ashore in Panama City while I stayed aboard as we were set to start our canal transit at midnight, and that was cutting it too close for me.

On the bridge at midnight the captain was complaining about my coffee. He wolfed down six cups in the first hour, then started to complain about it. There isn't any thing that tastes good after you've had that much of it (including prime rib). Some people are just not morning people.

At 0350 I turned over the bridge to the second mate and went back to the stern to handle lines. Vich relieved me on the stern at 0600, and I went in to finish work on the cargo papers, yeah, I still got stuck with them. There were two main cargo reports; the "TANKER ULLAGE AND CARGO REPORT, and the TANKER LOADING RECORD". The first, as the name indicates, is a record of the ullage taken at each tank top, and the calculations to arrive at the total number of barrels, and long tons of cargo at the standard temperature of 60 degrees Fahrenheit. For example; an ullage of 4 feet, 5 ½ inches in #5 Port Wing Tank, first has to be adjusted for the ship's trim as the tank top is at the rear of the tank. If the ship was loaded at even keel, the ullage would not change, but if the ship was loaded 4 inches down by the stern, that ullage would increase by ½ inch indicating ten less barrels of cargo for that tank. The corrected ullage is used in the ship's cargo tables to find the volume for the tank at that level; in this case indicating a volume of 12,124 barrels. Next we have to calculate the amount of water in the tank, which was 5 ½ inches as gauged by the surveyors.

Now that tank was pumped dry; I know because I stripped it, and the surveyors certified it as dry. So this water (and that's a lot of water – 115 barrels) came from the *RENOWN*. The problem here is not that they sold us water, we all knew about it, that's why each party has a witness to the gauging. So no one paid for water. However, that's 115 barrels of oil that we were not carrying, making the cargo we were carrying more expensive to transport. Any way, we now have 12,009 barrels of cargo in that tank at a recorded temperature of 82 degrees, that has to be converted to the standard temperature of 60 degrees, shrinking the volume more to 11899.7 barrels or 1661.97 long tons of cargo for that tank. (Incidentally, one barrel is 40 gallons, one long ton is 2240 pounds, and at 82 degrees, this oil was about 1161 barrels per long ton.) This had to be tabulated and calculated for each of our 15 tanks, and the resulting information was needed to fill out the second report.

The TANKER LOADING RECORD contained various ship's specifications like the Deadweight particulars, the draft at the loading port, the ship's fresh water allowance (indicating that the BC would sit 9 ¼ inches lower in the water in fresh water – like at Lake Charles which is far enough up river to be fresh, not salt water), amount of fresh water on board (for the crew and for the boilers), bunkers, or in short, every measurable consumable and the expected amount of consumables on board at reaching the destination. The object of this report is to calculate how much cargo can be loaded for the ship's present condition, to remain legal and safe on the way to and at the destination port. The bottom section is filled in from the other report and a few calculations are made to determine the loading rate and difference between what we are allowed to carry and what we are carrying. Fortunately, they always worked out well for me, or so I thought as we always seemed to have slightly less than the maximum. The proof, of course, was the ship's draft and how it sat by its plimsoll mark, an odd looking design on the side of every ship, governing the amount of cargo it can carry for the various waters of the world. This can be manipulated a bit, and I've seen it done, but most American operated ships followed the rules on this, because we all knew of cases where overloaded ships sank. These reports, as well as the loading and unloading of cargo are really the property of the chief mate and he carries the responsibility. A third mate should not have been running the operation or completing the reports.

    I stopped in for breakfast, and finished up the cargo papers before returning to the stern at 1000 for the lines at Gatun Locks. At noon, on the 11th we departed Cristobal and headed north for Lake Charles. Forty ships had transited the canal that day including eight American ships. Things were looking good. We were heading north in the Caribbean in good weather with a loaded and stable ship; I had plenty of work to keep me busy; I'd been to Colon, I didn't have to worry about locking my door, and I had my own private wading pool. Life was good.

Chapter 18

More of the Same

We were heading north. Panama was cooling off in the November weather with the sun at seventeen degrees south and going down, and the tropical storm season was closing out. Kendra had played out in the North Atlantic a week or so earlier and nothing had come to the Gulf or Caribbean since Greta. The Caribbean was in a tranquil mood with small glassy waves and no swell to speak of. Back home, New York was barren and getting cold, but I was far from it down there in the tropics. I can understand why people want to retire to the tropics where the weather is always warm, and snow is something these people can only imagine. I'd forgo the blizzards if I could do it without having to deal with the tropical storms. And I'd like the year round greenery if I didn't have to deal with all the bugs – there were a lot of bugs down here.

I put a 1600 DR position on the chart and was done for the watch. I played around with the RDF (radio direction finder) to see how accurate it was..not very. It was accurate enough for its day, but LORAN was better and easier to use. Each new generation of electronic navigational equipment is more accurate and easier to use than its predecessor. LORAN A was very accurate but was limited to coastwise navigation and had to be tuned for each station, LORAN C gave constant readings but with the same limitations, and Omega was on the horizon as a world wide system with constant read outs and no more dead space. We had no idea that we were on the verge of satellite navigation or GPS.

The radio traffic diminished as we steamed further north and by 1500 all was quiet, and we were quite alone in that expanse of the Caribbean with a thousand fathoms beneath the keel.

I performed my safety inspection that evening, noting which fire extinguishers had to be replaced the next day, and stopped by Marks office to pick up some times for the Port Log.

"Hey Chief."

"Uh, Tom...why is there always puddle of water outside your door?" he asked.

"A puddle of water? You want to know about the puddle of water?" I was incredulous. "I've had three inches of water in my room for a week and I can't seem to get any one to figure out why. When the ship rolls, it flows over the threshold into the passageway. That's why there's a puddle of water by the door."

"No one fixed the water yet?" He picked up the sound powered phone by his desk, set the dial to the engine room console, and turned the crank on the side. "This is Mark, is the 1st around?"

There was a pause, then he continued, "Hey Dick, this is Mark. There is still water in the third mates room....Yeah?.....Yeah?" Then to me he said, "He says you keep leaving the water running."

"Chief, do you think I'd leave the water running for a week? The valves are shut off. The water's coming up through the floor in the locker."

"Dick?...He says the valves are shut off and the water's coming up through the floor in the locker...Yeah?....Yeah?...." then to me again, "He says there are no pipes in your locker, the water can't be coming up there."

"Chief, we've mopped the room out a dozen times; the locker fills up, then overflows into the room. Then the room fills up and overflows into the passageway, where it flows under the door to the tween deck and disappears under the ladder. Someone's got to be able to figure out where all that water's coming from."

"Hey Dick...can you have someone take a look at it....Thanks. He says he'll have someone check it out. Is that what you wanted?"

"Actually I wanted the cargo times for the port log." He handed me a scrap of paper with some numbers scribbled on it. That's about all I ever got from him; I had to reverse engineer a lot of the numbers to make the logs match. It's no wonder he didn't want to make out the reports. In any case, if someone didn't plug that leak, I was going to have to get some rubber boots from the slop chest because that water was getting colder. I went back to my room and sat at my desk with my bare feet on the chair rung to keep out of the water. I filled in the times lightly in pencil so I would be able to make changes. It would have been a heck of a lot easier if I could have just put down what we actually did, instead of trying to write a good fiction. I finished for the evening and sloshed over to my bunk for a two-hour nap before taking the con.

I got up at my call and dried my feet in the passageway before donning my shoes and going down for a snack. I always checked the cereal for bugs after that one night, but hadn't seen any since then. Just the same, I always had the concern and exhibited the caution. I stopped on deck on my way back up and leaned on the railing for a few minutes. The sky was clear, and the seas calm. The turbulence from the bow washed back, boiling and hissing and fizzing. I started up the ladder to the tween deck and passed through the port and back to the ladder in the dark, looking for the crack of light beneath the door. I could hear the wind whistling under the door. It didn't sound like voices that night, except maybe a few...

Vich was rip roaring mad that night when I relieved him on the bridge. At first I couldn't understand what he was crabbing about; something about "that stupid Limey" and "I was here first" and "mind his own business". He kept complaining about someone and it sounded like he had a bit of traffic that did not sit well with him. It took a few minutes for him to get composed enough to get his story out. This is what took place, as far as I could figure it out.

Vich was steering our standard departure course of 348, heading toward the Quito Sueno Bank, still a half day away, when a ship appeared on his starboard bow. The aspect of the ship indicated that it would be crossing, but the relative bearing remained the same as the two ships closed on each other, indicating that they were on a collision course. This was a textbook rules of the road case. This is what should have happened.

The other ship had the right of way because it was on the starboard bow of the BC; and the BC was the give way vessel because it was on the port bow of the other ship. Vich should have altered his course to starboard, early enough and widely enough to be visibly apparent to the other ship, allowing the other ship to maintain its course and speed, as required by the rules of the road, and passing ahead of the BC. Vich would have taken the BC under the stern of the other ship and then changed his course back to 348.

But what actually happened is probably more like this. Vich was steady on 348. The other ship appeared on the horizon to starboard as stated previously. Vich assumed that he had the right of way. (I don't know why, it might have been a brain cloud, or a control panel malfunction.) Vich took no action and kept his course and speed. When the ships became dangerously close and the officer of the other ship saw no action being taken by Vich, He probably called Vich on the radio with a very English accent, saying something like this..

"This is the *STALWART*, 120 miles north of Cristobal calling the ship in my vicinity, on my port bow, heading north. I am on your starboard bow at about five miles."

Vich probably responded with, "This is the *BALTIMORE CANON* back to the *STALWART*."

"*BALTIMORE CANON* can you please tell me your intentions? Will you be altering your course to starboard?"

"Hey *STALWART* I'm not going around you, I was here first. You're the one who came over the horizon. You go around me."

"Very good sir, if you will maintain your course, I will go in behind you."

"Of course I'm going to keep on my course, I've been steering this course all night, and I'm going to keep on steering it. Who do you think you are?"

"Very good sir, *STALWART* out."

Now, that sounds ridiculous; but as far as I could tell, that's pretty close to what happened. The words and phrases came from Vich himself as he was trying to explain to me what happened. I figure the English officer realized right away what the problem was and got out of it as expediently as possible. I think Vich started to realize for himself what happened as he worked through it, trying to get me to understand why he was so mad at the Englishman. By the time he went below I think he knew.

Well, we all go through life changing experiences, and this was one for me. When I got below at 0400, I took off my shoes, stepped into my pool, and immediately gathered my lifeboat clothing (all white) and lifeboat necessities (life jacket, knife, can opener, string, flashlight, waterproof matches, etc.). I loaded the pockets and hung the clothes on the hook next to my door, with the lifejacket over them. I wanted to be ready to go. I had a captain who was wanted in Panama, a chief mate who didn't seem to know much about cargo, a second mate who smoked dope, an old third mate who was now confused, and a ghost hovering over me in the chart room. Add to that, five engineers who couldn't get through a single voyage without using at least fifteen fire extinguishers, none of whom could figure out why I had three inches of water in my room. If that ship didn't sink or ground or blow up, someone was going to accidentally scuttle it. From that morning on, twenty-five years ago, I have not been able to sleep through a night. To this day, I wake every hour or two, listen for a while to make sure everything's okay, and doze off for another hour or so.

Chapter 19

Apprehension

I was glad that I was on the bridge for rounding Quito Sueno. I was still apprehensive from the previous night, and only seemed to feel comfortable when I was on the bridge. The small fishing boats were strung out along the banks again. I couldn't see the big boat. These guys were a long way from anywhere.

We passed Misteriosa on noon of the 13th. Someone found a shallower spot than I did a few years later. If I'd have found that one, I would have ripped the bottom out of the BC because it was only thirty-five feet deep. That would have made the papers.

The next two days were relaxing with good weather, electronic navigation and little traffic. On the morning of the 16th, we anchored in the gulf outside of Calcasieu Pass to wait for the tide. It seemed a storm had blown through a few days earlier and part of the channel got filled in with sand and silt. Apparently this is a normal thing in the gulf. At 1210 we pulled the hook and proceeded in to the pass, but I think we rushed it a little because we were in trouble by1500. Around 1505 the ship started to vibrate a little which was unusual for us in our loaded condition. I stepped out on to the port wing and looked around and saw a lot of muddy water being churned up behind us. At 1510 our progress was very slow, and at 1520, the BC heeled to port and stopped forward progress. I put the engines on stop; we were aground. We were in the middle of the channel, but we were aground.

We waited. The tide was still coming in and we hoped it would be enough to float us. Can you imagine that? We did everything right, and we still grounded. And all we could do was wait and hope. We were on a fifteen million dollar ship, hoping that nature would fix a problem that nature had a hand in causing - and we weren't disappointed. By 1620, the tide was high enough to float us off, and with the engines on slow ahead, we resumed our way up the channel. That was just about the time we lost the Force Draft Blower, a mechanical device that provides the huge volume of air required by the boilers for complete combustion of the fuel oil. One thing for sure, the BC was consistent. It was consistently a disaster. On reflection, I can understand why the engineers couldn't fix my water problem; they couldn't get out of the engine room long enough to catch their breath!

Eventually, we got up the river and docked. I had 23 fire extinguishers next to the gangway to be recharged. The captain had ordered a night mate so we could go ashore for the night, but the chief restricted me to the ship to work cargo anyway. There wasn't much point to that as the tanks were full and it would be twelve hours before anyone had to do anything, but there I was, stuck aboard with the night mate.

After my noon watch, I ducked out with Bob to get some shore time. I felt a little guilty about it because I knew they would have to start stripping tanks in the next hour or so, but I figured I could deal with that when I got back. As it turned out, they had great success on their own and I didn't have to deal with it at all. In Lake Charles I bought a seven-band radio with some short wave frequencies. I hadn't heard any music or news in five months. At 0100 we shifted out to the anchorage to await bunkers. I called the engine room around 0230 for the barge and it looked like a 0500 sailing.

Getting out of that river was a lot easier than getting in as we were no longer constrained by our draft. The gulf crossing was quiet and all was well until we lost one of the boilers just south of Misteriosa Bank. We continued on to the Gorda Bank at half speed where the engineers completed temporary repairs and we proceeded at full sea speed around Quito Sueno.

Heading south along Quito Sueno Bank I saw a ship to port heading west, right toward the bank, no more than ten miles off. I called them on the radio to see what they were doing.

"This is the *BALTIMORE CANON* calling the ship in my vicinity along the Quito Sueno Bank about ten miles to the east. I am directly ahead of you." There was no answer. I repeated the call, again with no success. So I tried my broken Spanish.

"Esta el *BALTIMORE CANON* llamando el barco al porto a las dies miles de Quito Sueno." Which meant something close to what I said in English, I think. And I got a response, but I don't think Spanish was his first language either, which made the whole mess all the more convoluted. It went something like this.

"Hola, estamos *Rivera Mediterraneo*." (Hello, we are the Mediterranean River.)?

"*Rivera Mediterraneo*, adonde va?" (*River Mediterranean*, where are you going?)

"Este...eh..Vamos al Puerto Cabezas. Adonde va?" (We go to Puerto Cabezas. Where are you going?)

I went into the chartroom and looked at the chart. Puerto Cabezas was on the coast directly on the other side of the bank. It looked like they were headed straight across the bank; they'd never make it. There are rocks that break the surface at low tide.

I got back on the radio. "Vamos al Canal Panama, pero usted no va al Puerto Cabezas de aqui; necessito va al sur. No hay agua en Quito Sueno. Va al sur." (We are going to the Panama Canal, but you cannot go to Puerto Cabezas from here. You need to go to south. There is no water on Quito Sueno. Go to the south.)

"No, no, vamos al Puerto Cabezas, vamos con los otro barcos." (No, we go to Puerto Cabezas, we go with the other ships.)

"No no, no. Los otro barcos estan en la terra. No hay agua alla. No va con los barcos, va veinte cuatro miles al Sur, entonces va al Puerto Cabeza. (No, the other ships are on land. There is no water there. Don't go with those ships. Go twenty-four miles south, then go to Puerto Cabezas.)

"Si, si, comprendo. No agua alla por los barcos. Vamos al sur. Gracias. Vamos al sur" (Yes, we understand, there is no water by the ships. We go south.")

I'm sure that's not exactly how it went, but it's as close as I can remember. They must have understood something because they turned south and traveled along with us for a while, before turning west. But what if we hadn't lost that boiler when we did? We'd have been gone from this area, and there might now be five ships on that reef.

We anchored in Limon Bay, inside the breakwaters on the 23rd, and I caught the 2000 launch in with Kevin. We were more careful with our selections that evening, and did stop in for a drink with some of the crew. When we got back to the dock, we found six or eight cases of booze and cigars waiting for our launch, and the chief mate standing guard. This was unusual for two reasons. First, booze isn't allowed on American ships. Oh, I know, there's always some around somewhere; but not out and in your face, as in six cases. Second, who would need six cases of booze and two cases of cigars?

When the launch came in, they loaded the cases and the rest of the crew got on. Then, some customs official came aboard and wanted to know who owned the goods. The dock supervisor pointed to the chief mate, so the customs agent asked him who he was, because the duty would have to be paid on that quantity. The chief mate told him that he was the chief engineer on the BALTIMORE CANON. Well, we didn't want anyone to get arrested so we kept our mouth shut, and saved it until we saw the chief engineer. This guy was going to be trouble.

We were only there for about twenty-four hours but that was enough to keep the crew happy, and get the chief engineer into trouble.

We left the evening of the 24th and went strait in to the RENOWN. The chief called me out early again to get the de-ballasting underway. (I don't think he liked de-ballasting.) I got it going and ran it through my watch. They should have finished up around 1800, but when I went out at 2350, they still had five feet left in #5 center tank. I finished that out and ran around with the surveyor, then lined up for loading. I was called out again after dinner to do the cargo survey. I suppose it was better that I did the survey, because then I had the numbers, otherwise I might have had to fudge that too.

By midnight we were anchored in Balboa, heading north by late morning, and leaving the canal behind by 1600 on the 27th. I didn't see any new wrecks on Quito Sueno so the *RIVER MEDITERRANEAN* must have gotten by it. I don't know what they were using for charts, but that bank has been on charts for a hundred years.

There seemed to be a lot of typing required on this voyage; crew lists, radio relays, stores, cargo papers etc. My original plan included not being behind a desk. Captain Daniels was planning to pay the crew off again in Lake Charles, and that meant more paperwork.

The weather in the gulf turned nasty. It rained continuously on the 30th and the 1st of December brought thunder, lightning and heavy rain all morning and afternoon. Visibility was poor and the radar was on continuously. We entered Calcasieu Pass in heavy rain and had no difficulty as they had dredged the channel while we were down south. The ship paid off at 1800 on the 2nd. I stayed but Vich went home.

Around 0400, one of the ABs boarded, fleeing from a cabbie, and disappeared back in the house. Kevin paid the cabbie. I got an early call to do another arrival slip (the last story wasn't good enough.), fill out some vouchers and then I had to take the utility messman to the hospital. After watch I had to do more work on the crew lists; due to the crew changeovers; and sooner or later the fat fingers routine was going to be called.

I was twenty minutes late for watch on the morning of the 4th, the first time I slept in, in five months. That's right, December 4th, I was now a short timer, one month, four prime ribs, and eight bars of soap to go.

We finished cargo and ballast, crewed up and departed by 1600 that day, heading south for a somewhat different voyage. There was traffic in the fairway that night but nothing too heavy. The weather had blown itself out and was calm but still cloudy. The stars were out in the morning, and traffic all but disappeared when we exited the traffic fairway. John stopped by for a few seconds, just to check on me I suppose. Although I expected it, it was still a little unnerving, and I still caught a small chill. I had another new watch. The preacher had gotten off on his standard emphysema routine, Robel had back problems and Menendez moved to the 4-8 watch taking Sunnto's place so he could get more overtime.

My present helmsman was Tex, (of course from Texas), at 6'2", 220 pounds and long red curly hair (long meaning about four inches past his shoulders). Tex wore tee shirts, short shorts, a cowboy hat and cowboy boots, exclusively. He seemed to be a good natured, "good ol' boy", strong, daring, and a show off. Sundi, my other new AB was a polar opposite; short (about 5') squat, dark skinned, short dark hair and maybe a half dozed teeth left. Sundi was a great fisherman. My new ordinary, Nick, was a young kid, probably twenty, tall, thin, curly blond hair, and this was his first ship. I tried out the ABs on hand steering for a while until I was satisfied, but I held off on Nick. Until I could train him, he couldn't stand a wheel watch.

We went by Cuba in the afternoon of the 6th, and were passing Misteriosa Bank at midday on the 7th when we lost the boiler again. These were not good waters to be on one boiler; the currents would have twice the effect. We had to steer 127 to keep off Gorda Bank, and it seemed to take forever to get to Quito Sueno. For five months we had traveled at fifteen knots in our light condition, and certain expectations developed about where we would be and when. We were now doing eight, making seven good with the current. Try taking your car out on the highway and traveling at thirty miles an hour; see how long you can take it. The weather also had a greater effect on us. Seas that were small and had no significant effect on us at fifteen knots, now carried us with them, not too badly, but enough to require soaking down the tablecloths again, enough to provide the soothing sounds of the shore while I tried to sleep, and enough to keep the passageway outside of my room awash. The good news was that the vibration had stopped at the lower speed, the bad news? I was pretty much on my own with the flooding.

Quito Sueno was visible during my whole watch and the canal, which should have been a day away, was going to be twice that. I sighted Cristobal in the afternoon of the 10th, two days that felt more like babysitting the BC, hoping that nothing else would go wrong, than operating a tank ship. We anchored that evening, and I stood another idyllic anchor watch in Limon Bay, checking anchor bearings, standing by for the launch, reading, and occasionally looking around to see if I could find another bug like the Geep. I didn't need one, but that was an interesting time, and he would now be in his native habitat – a swamp. Kevin went ashore and returned at 0415 for watch.

We were kind of suspended there, waiting to shift over to the dock for repairs. Some of the tubes had burned out in the boiler and had to be plugged. The engineer's needed dock time for that, because there was going to be a lot of comings and goings. As far as I knew, burned out tubes were caused by not keeping enough water in the boiler, allowing the tubes to over heat. I'm sure there was also an age factor, and the BC was, well, I think I covered that earlier. I didn't speculate then, and I won't now, as to whom or what caused the problem, as I wasn't an engineer, and wasn't intimately involved in trying to keep that steam plant operational. I also wasn't privy to the discussions about what needed to be done or how long it would take.

We shifted to the dock at 2130, locked the bridge and moved the watch to the gangway, officially, waiting for repairs.

Chapter 20

Repairs

Repairs started on the 12th. I loaded twelve tins of plastic for the boiler; that is twelve, two hundred pound tins of plastic. There were also plugs, pipes and pallets of other materials. With our delay, the chief engineer was granted permission by the company to have his wife join him on the ship for the duration. It was starting to look like a lot more than plugging a few pipes.

While materials were being delivered over the next few days, another storm was brewing, not with the weather, with the chief mate. His activities were starting to come to light.

I went ashore the morning of the 13th to do some shopping. I wanted to get a Panama hat to wear on deck in the sun, and as we were alongside, we could come and go as we pleased as long as we covered our watches. At the gate I pointed to one of the shore pilots and waved him over. He looked like he just won the lottery, in fact he had.

"Quiero comprar un sombrero Panama. Sabe adonde vamos?" I was asking, in my best Spanish where to by a Panama hat.

"Si, yo se, va conmigo, my friend, come, I show." He replied, and we were off zigzagging through the streets dodging traffic. In less than ten minutes we entered a small neatly kept hat shop and the proprietor greeted us.

"Hola, como estas?"

"Bien, puede heche un sombrero para me?" I was using words I remembered from my school days. I knew it was more like castillian Spanish, not the local version, but I figured they'd get the drift. What's the worst that could happen? I might end up with goat cheese or something. The man walked over to one of the counters on which were displayed different styles, and I selected one that looked similar to a fedora. Then he pointed to the different hat bands, and I chose one of them. He motioned me to come closer, and produced a tape measure, which he wrapped around my head.

"Cinco horas" he said.

That was five hours. I would be on duty then. I pointed at my watch. "A las cinco?" I asked.

"Si, a las cinco."

"Quantos dinero?" I needed to know how much it would be.

"Treintycinco" He responded. I paid him and went outside.

"Espera" My pilot said to me, and he went back in the store. "Commisione, commisione" I heard him say to the proprietor. He got himself a commission on my purchase, good for him. He wanted to know where else I wanted to go.

"Where to go, my friend?"

"Quiero comprar una camisa, que los pilotos tiene." I wanted to get the kind of shirt the canal pilots wore but I didn't know what they were called so I tried to explain it with hand gestures.

"Si, I know, you come." And we were off again.

He did know. I shopped around for a few hours until I had to return for watch. I left him at the gate with a few extra dollars.

Back on board, the new third mate told me the captain was looking for me, so I stopped by his office after lunch. There was a problem with the chief mate. He asked me about all the overtime for cargo operations and cargo papers. I explained, as well as I could about all of the paper work from both the chief mate and himself with the port papers, and that normally I wouldn't be doing that work, as it wasn't the third mate's job. There was also the matter of the cargo work that was requested by the chief mate. He agreed with me and acknowledged that they had off loaded some of their work, and that the chief mate wasn't handling his responsibilities very well. The problem wasn't my overtime, it was the chief mate's. The company had reviewed his overtime reports had had come to the conclusion that to get as much overtime as he claimed, he had to work 23 hours a day for one week, and 24 hours a day for the other three weeks in the month. That being the case, why did he need me to help him with his work? Well, I couldn't explain that, and the captain knew it. Apparently, the chief used a loophole in the union contract that allowed a day worker to sleep during his normal day time hours, if he had worked overtime through the night. He simply changed his work hours to the night so he would be paid while he slept during the day putting him on the clock, so to speak, 24 hours a day. I couldn't help the captain with that one, and I was due on deck, so I had to leave.

We loaded more plastic that afternoon, and the chief engineer was negotiating for dry ice. They needed to freeze the plugs to shrink them before pounding them in so they would expand in place. The problem was that there was no supplier of dry ice in Cristobal or Colon. The nearest supplier was in Panama City at the other end of the canal, fifty miles away. That might not be a problem in a temperate climate with an interstate highway and refrigerated trucks, but this was the tropics, the highway was two lanes with slow traffic, and refrigerated trucks hadn't been invented down there yet; so this was going to be a challenge.

I went in at 1600 to pick up my hat, and after trying it on, ordered another for the next day. It was so light and pliable that I couldn't tell I had it on. I wore it the rest of the afternoon. I stopped in several places and had a few drinks with the guys, returning to the ship around 2100. The scuttlebutt was that the captain was negotiating something with the chief mate. The chief was a sly one though so I guessed who'd get the better bargain.

The ice started showing up on the 14th. It was one of the sillier things I'd seen. There was a steady stream of Panamanians coming up the gangway with satchels over their shoulders, carrying the dry ice. Apparently, the satchels were filled in Panama City and given to these carriers who were transported by vans to Cristobal, where they got out and carried the satchels to the ship and down to the engine room boilers. There must have been two or three hundred of these guys because they formed a never-ending line. The satchels were loaded with about a cubic foot of dry ice each, but by the time they crossed the isthmus, got down to the boiler and opened the bags, something about the size of a golf ball, was all that was left. This continued for about 24 hours before they threw in the towel and decided to come up with a better method.

Meanwhile, the deal with the chief mate was sealed. The chief would stay aboard and work with no overtime pay until he paid the company back what he stole. I couldn't see this happening but that was the deal.

We loaded some degreaser for the *RENOWN*, on the 15th, so I guessed they were optimistic about our repairs. On the morning of the 16th, at 0215, one of the gate guards came to the bottom of the gangway and wanted to know where the chief engineer was. I told him I didn't know, but he was probably in his room sleeping. The guard started up the gangway with his gun drawn, and I stopped him right there.

"Stop." He did.

"I've got a girl at the gate out there with no pants on, who says the chief engineer didn't pay her and stole her pants." He explained.

"First, you're not allowed on this ship. The only law officer allowed on a United States Merchant Ship uninvited is a United States Marshall, so get back on the dock. Second, if the chief engineer is aboard, then he's been aboard all night because he hasn't been on deck since I've had the watch. He also has his wife aboard, so he can't be the one you are looking for."

"Just the same, he has to come out to the gate and settle this."

"Wait on the dock, I'll call him." I sent Nick in to call the chief engineer on deck without explaining, in case his wife was listening; but I already had an idea of what happened. This was another of the chief mate's messes. They both had an average build, and both had short dark hair and beards, and I'd already heard him give the chief engineer's name in another incident. The chief engineer came out to the gangway.

"What is going on out here?"

"I'm sorry about this Chief, but the gate guard is on the dock looking for you. Someone skipped out on a local business woman and then stole her clothes figuring she wouldn't follow. I know it's not you, and when she sees you she'll tell him. But you'll have to go with him."

"Tex, you go with him and make sure nothing happens to him." Tex stood up tall and stretched his muscles.

"Don't worry Mate. I'll take care of him." I knew Tex was hoping that something would happen, and I was just slightly worried that Tex would start something if someone else didn't; but I was willing to take the risk.

When they had gone about 100 feet from the gangway I turned to Nick. "Nick, you see how far away they are? Keep that distance. If any thing happens, get back here fast. And if you see any of your ship mates coming back, have them hang around until we have the chief back." Nick bounded down the gangway.

They weren't gone long. When the girl saw him, she knew she'd been had. That was the risk in her game. Many are the sailors that have lost a month's wages in one night with these girls, and every once in a while it backfired on the girl. Oh, the indignity of it!

Later that morning, the ice contractor arrived with the solution to the problem. He had newly designed containers for the ice and it would be arriving in a few hours. So every one got back in gear, and the ice arrived in the new containers. They looked just like the old ones except the new ones were "insulated". Well when the ice arrived, there was an improvement, now they had something the size of a small snowball. So in came three hundred snowballs, one at a time. Either it was enough to get the job done, or they came up with another way because that's the last I saw of dry ice.

The engine room stores arrived but the bosun was nowhere around so I had to deal with it myself. There was also another missing person; the chief mate had flown the coop. I guess he wasn't going to pay the company back.

There was a lot of activity with the engine repairs on the 17th; it looked like we would be sailing soon. I was glad; most of the crew was broke and trying to borrow money. The girls had cleaned them all out. On the morning of the 18th, I set the sailing board for 1600. I tested the gear at 1530 and warmed up the radar unit for the pilot. With the pilot aboard and the tug alongside, we lifted the gangway onto the deck.

"Single up for and aft" the pilot suggested and the captain gave the order.

When the breast lines alone held us, the pilot asked to let go for and aft.

I logged last line.

"Slow Ahead" requested the pilot.

"Slow Ahead" I repeated, moving the EOT handle to Slow Ahead. The bell rang momentarily as the Engineer matched my setting. I watched the RPM indicator, counting quietly, 1...2..3..4..5... "We have no RPMS yet." I waited another five seconds. "Still no RPMS" I repeated. I strode over to the phone, set the dial to Engine Console and cranked the handle. A muffled voice answered. "Engine Room"

I cupped my hand over the mouth piece and loudly stated "We've got no RPMs."

"I know, we got a problem with the generator."

"Okay, put her on stop" I told him.

The EOT started ringing. I walked over and matched the Stop setting the engineer had set his telegraph to. "Captain, they've got a problem with the generator."

The problem was that the generator burned up. We were dead in the water. A conference was held on the bridge, with the shore on the radio, and the engine room on the phone. There was a reason we couldn't stay at the dock (it might have been financial), so we were towed out to anchor in Limon Bay, and the second mate went forward to anchor the ship. More parts were delivered by launch for the engine room that evening and still more the next day. Early on the 20th, with temporary repairs to the generator, we acted on orders to proceed to Curacao at whatever speed we could make, for repairs in the shipyard on that island.

We'd spent ten days in Panama. It wasn't bad being paid to hang around the deck, with little responsibility and less work. We had to tend the lines, but there was only a three-foot tide, requiring no real work. We did have to watch for boarders, but the only attempt had been the gate guard. This had been a lazy ten days for the deck crew. On the other hand, the engineers were put to the task. It had been a grueling time for them, and it wasn't over. I don't think they missed much in Colon though.

The city was busy and dirty, with bugs and vermin out of control. The people themselves were rather dirty and looked quite ragged for all the money they were fleecing the sailors of. The crew of the BC must have dropped thirty thousand dollars on that town in ten days, and that was just one ship, and those sailors had absolutely nothing to show for it. Most of the stores were run by Indians (from India), and they were not inexpensive, although haggling was common. Aldaos, the hat place was expensive for the area, and I bought two, because they were good hats, and custom fit; but the locals could never afford that. The bars were mostly dimly lit houses of ill repute, and at each, we were met by ladies of the evening at the door – even in the afternoon. Drinks cost a dollar fifty, equal to about three hour's wages for the locals. The only respectable places I found were the VIP Bar and Restaurant, and the Yacht Club, which was reserved for members only, or by invitation – the way I got in.

It's not really safe to walk the streets alone; you're safer in company or with a trustworthy shore pilot who will take you wherever you want to go, for a small commission. The working girls were mostly Columbian (a loose arrangement) providing contract services with standardized fees based on the time of day; but I think their big money came from handouts from drunken sailors. They dressed nicely and were mostly clean, but if you didn't want to be bothered, you just let them know that you had no money and they would flee from you like you had the plague. On the other hand, any sailor that pulled out a wad of money was set upon like black fly season in the Adirondacks. The town is mostly a trap for seamen and tourists. Ten days was too long for a port like that.

Chapter 21

More Repairs

On December 20 we departed Limon Bay, headed for Curacao at whatever speed we could make, which was a little over half speed. It was good to break loose of that money pit. I was glad I got to see it, but I'd had enough and some of the crew now owed money to the captain for advances against their future wages. Hopefully, the shipyard in Curacao was better equipped to handle twentieth century problems.

Curacao was one of the Dutch Antilles in the southern Caribbean about forty miles north of Venezuela. The three main islands, called the ABC islands, (Aruba, Bonaire, and Curacao) all had oil terminals; Dutch Royal Shell operated on Curacao. Business was booming in the oil business with the manufactured oil shortages, driving the price of oil up in the seventies and early eighties. It would be a few years yet before finance and industry would discover the fraud, and the economies of islands like these (and these specifically) would collapse in what the world would call an oil glut.

But for the present, their economies were growing at a fantastic rate; while we proceeded at a snail's pace (without a chief mate) to the shipyard at the central island, Curacao. We took care of the small stuff, fire and boat drill, safety inspection, and port log, (no cargo papers this time) while we trudged along, hoping the engineers could keep us moving. Sometimes it seemed as though they were hand cranking the propeller shaft, because we were barely making any headway. We had a Fire and Boat Drill on the afternoon of the 22nd. I got the port side boat, and was not happy with the confusion in the crew, I had some work to do to get this procedure ironed out. The weather was good to us; and traffic consisted mostly of small coasters and fishing boats. I was on deck with maintenance and repair in the mornings, safety work in the afternoons (I had to inspect the lifeboat equipment – there's a lot of stuff in the lifeboats.) and paper work in the evenings. On the 23rd, the second mate advanced the clocks an hour as we crawled east into the next time zone. Later that day we passed between Aruba and the Peninsula de Paraguana of Venezuela. There were a lot of ships anchored off that peninsula.

We approached Curacao at midnight and hove to, while waiting for entry information. At noon we started in. The island is small and the channel into the inner harbor is narrow. The city of Willemstad straddles the channel with a movable pontoon bridge that swings open to let ships pass. There was fixed bridge over this same channel that rose to a height of 170 feet. (I think it's still there.) It looked like the highest thing on the island. From my perch in the wheelhouse of the BC in light condition, Willemstad looked like a toy town, seventy feet below me on either side. The BC looked too big to go through the channel, and I checked the mast as we went under the fixed bridge. Of course we weren't too big or too high. The BC was a small tanker; there was plenty of room for ships larger then us.

At 1330 the captain called fore and aft. Kevin went forward and I went aft, leaving Dan, the new third mate on the bridge. After Captain Daniels called ALL FAST, he called me to the bridge on the radio. I had to fill out the crew list and customs papers before knocking off. I was in terrible shape that evening with a bad headache, dizziness, cramps and nausea. I hadn't been getting much sleep, waking every hour or so. And there had been a lot of work to do. I had probably been working on three hours of sleep a day, an hour at a time. I took the midnight gangway watch and didn't get relieved until 0755. I was a dead man walking. I went up to my room, opened the door, walked in soaking my shoes, and collapsed on my rack. My head was pounding.

I couldn't sleep for the incessant pounding in my head, or was it on my door. Someone was pounding on my door. I pushed off the rack into the water, staggered over to the door and swung in opened. It was Dan.

"You look like hell."

"I feel like hell."

"Can you stand watch?"

"What time is it?"

"1215"

"Already? I just got here. Yeah, just give me a minute to get into something dry." I closed the door and turned around, too fast, and fell. What a bracer! Now I was really wet. I changed into some dry clothes, put my wet shoes on the dresser and took the dry ones out into the passageway with a towel. This was getting old; I'd been flooded for six weeks. That poor BR had been mopping out that mess every day for six weeks. On the up side, I had the cleanest deck on the ship.

I worked my way down to the gangway and sat down on one of the cargo pipes. I still felt lousy. There was a lot of traffic at the gangway, and the noise seemed to be bouncing between my ears. I closed my eyes for a few seconds. When I opened them, the messman was standing in front of me holding a bag.

"You missed dinner." He stated.

"Dinner?... Oh, that's right, I slept through lunch."

"It's Christmas Day, you missed Christmas dinner." He continued.

"Christmas?" I didn't get what he was saying. "What day is it?"

"It's December 25, Christmas Day, and you missed Christmas dinner. Cook put out a nice spread."

"Christmas..?" It didn't seem like Christmas. It was hot... I'm not normally so slow. It was the fever, or lack of sleep, the exhaustion. But it soon came to me. I hadn't ever thought about Christmas in the tropics. In New York, at this time of the year, it's cold; there's snow on the ground. The merchants have been playing Christmas music since Thanksgiving, trying to get customers to part with their money. There were decorations all over and there were lights on the houses at night. Down here, Christmas quietly slipped in without the music, without the lights, without the gifts. We were so busy with our problems for the last month that I didn't much think about anything, other than staying afloat.

"Yes, it's Christmas, Merry Christmas." I said.

"When you didn't come down, I packed you some dinner" he said, handing the bag to me.

"Thanks, I appreciate that." I didn't have the heart to tell him that I was nauseous, and couldn't eat anything (of all days). I put the bag down next to me. "I guess I'll have dinner in a few minutes, when it quiets down, thanks."

He went down the gangway for a few hours ashore, and I struggled to keep vigilant for the next few hours on deck. I took my lunch up to my room when Kevin came out on deck. I was still out of it. I remembered to take my shoes off that time, and waded over to my rack and crashed again. I had nothing at all to eat on Christmas Day.

I got my 2330 call and went out on deck for a 12-hour gangway watch. We changed our hours to 12 on 12 off for the day so we could all get ashore. I felt better; it must have been one of those 24-hour bugs.

The captain woke me early on the 27th to do some work on the stress tables. These are used for calculations for hog and sag in loaded or ballast conditions. This would be something in the chief mate's area, but of course, we didn't have a chief mate. So I worked on these until watch at noon, and went out on deck. But the captain sent Dan down to take the deck watch and put me back to work on the calculations. Without any records of our ballast history, I had to figure out how much to take on and where to keep it. I knew what we had been doing, but that wasn't good enough; we had to know why.

I ducked out at noon on the 28th with Kevin before any one could grab me, and we went in for some refreshment. But before we got to a watering hole I had to take care of some other business. I'd been aboard almost six months, and this was probably to be my last voyage. I wanted some good clothes to go home in, and most of what I'd brought had been ruined for that purpose. So my first stop was a clothing store. I bought a good pair of pants and a good shirt, but the pants needed to be hemmed and the store didn't provide that service. I asked around, and was sent to a seamstress on one of the side streets. She had me try them on and stand on the platform so she could pin them, then told me to come back for them in three days. I couldn't wait three days; we might be gone by then, so she agreed to have them ready for me in three hours (very accommodating). I went back at 1600 and they were ready. The charge was three dollars, so I gave her a five; but she said she had no change. I explained that I only had two singles but I would be happy to give her the five. She declined and accepted the two singles (what a deal). I think she wanted the American money, and would take less to get it. She was also probably too honest to take more than she earned. I thanked her and went down the street to look for a cab. We went to the Holiday Inn on the other side of the channel for a couple of hours. It was small, but a nice place. Besides the fresh water swimming pool, it had a small lagoon walled off from the ocean to keep the sharks out. I made a mental note to wear my swim suit the next time came this way. I had no idea that I'd actually be back at this hotel within a year. We returned to the ship at 1900, so I could get some shut-eye, as I had the midnight watch. But I got called an hour later to do the payroll. That wasn't even close to being my job. I worked on that until my watch at midnight.

The 29th was a restful day with just 12 hours on deck. I guess all the other work was completed to the captain's satisfaction because he didn't bother me that day. On the 30th, our schedules were back to normal. The repairs were just about complete and we had to prepare to take the ship back into service. The sailing board was set for noon, and shortly after that we shifted to Pier 5 for bunkers. We took departure at 2200 and headed west-southwest to Panama.

There is a strange phenomenon on board ships that has to do with perceived experience. An officer of any rank, joining a ship is treated as unaccomplished and suspect, until he demonstrates in some way that he knows what he's doing. Every one watches him, and waits. The deck crew knows an officer by the way he comes up the gangway, and can tell within a few minutes if he knows what he's doing. But with the officers, it takes a lot longer, sometimes weeks, sometimes until another officer is replaced, to take the heat. On the other hand, an officer who is on board prior to a new replacement is treated like a seasoned officer by the joining officer, even if he only preceded him by a week.

I'd been aboard the longest, and was treated as the most experienced even though this was my first ship. I had filled in for the chief mate on several occasions even though we had a second, and had been made responsible for the ships papers and payroll on the assumption that I was a well seasoned officer, (though I was the greenest aboard), based entirely on the fact that I was there first. This is not an observation based solely on my time on the BC, but on my experience over the years on all of the ships I sailed. I would always hope the other officers were about to change over after I joined, so I would not be in the hot seat for long.

Chapter 22

The Caretaker

The crew had been in a lackadaisical and hopeless mood for the last week. It seemed that the ship was just slowly falling apart and could no longer play a useful role in the oil business. For the last few months, it seemed as though one thing after another failed, and the ship was not destined to continue. This was not the case. Some companies simply milk a business without any reinvestment of capital, in effect using up the business as a consumable. These people are international corporate locusts, buying, using, and casting away, with no intention of running or building a healthy business. The shipping industry is not immune to this type of operation and the *BALTIMORE CANON* was one of the consumables that these corporate locusts bought. They were using her up; band aids and patches were all she was going to get. So, on leaving Curacao, the crew was a bit apprehensive about the ship's actual condition, and whether she would make port in Panama. Of course, she would, on one of the strangest voyages I have ever had and this night would be the one to make it so.

I took the con at 2345 on a moonless night heading to a point midway between Aruba and Venezuela, with a long low swell coming in on the starboard beam that gave us an easy roll. On the chart, the second mate (also known as the navigator) had the track laid to a point between the two that we would reach at about 0200, at which time we would change our course to 278 to steam west north west, rounding Columbia, before heading south west to Panama.

Around 0100, heading into that narrow area (narrow for the sea but about fifteen miles wide), we were in traffic with two ships on our port side, converging, with steady relative bearings. That makes three of us on a collision course. This was not a problem for us as we were the right of way ship, as long as the other two ships followed the rules of the road. In a case like this, we were required to keep our course and speed so the others would know what to do. However, of the other two ships, one was the right of way ship which was also required to keep his course and speed in relation to the other. So the middle ship was required to both keep his course and speed and to adjust one or the other at the same time. Again, this is not a problem, as seasoned officers know that nothing in the rules requires them to put themselves into danger, and the rules mandate that we depart from the rules if following them would cause such a situation.

What worried me was that many foreign ships have only one licensed officer on the ship, and the others are someone's brothers, or cousins. I was verifying our position every fifteen minutes to make sure I knew exactly where we were in the event that I had to maneuver out of the situation. At 0122, I was looking at the radar screen, when harsh white light flooded onto the bridge. I spun around, dashed into the chartroom and flipped the red filter back onto the chart table light, twisting the thumbscrews to tighten it. Somehow that filter had come loose. I thought it just hadn't been tightened earlier. White light is bad on the bridge at night as it ruins the crew's night vision. It's also bad in traffic at night because it gives off additional lighting, which could confuse other ships in the area. I looked down at the chart, picked up the pencil and put it between the triangles so it wouldn't roll off. But as I stepped through the door to the bridge, the filter came off the light again, flooding the bridge with the harsh white light. I went back and re-secured the light, checking the screws and making sure the filter was tight. I looked at the chart. The pencil was lying on the chart by itself. I could feel John; he was there right behind me. "Oh, we're right here." I said, placing a spot on the chart and labeling it 0122. I put the pencil between the triangles again, then stepped onto the bridge to get away from him; I had other problems that night. But he didn't go.

As I was stepping through the door, he whistled, the kind of whistle that says, "Hey, come here." I looked back. Then I looked at Tex, who was steering.

"Did you hear anything?" I asked Tex.

"Yeah Mate, someone whistled for you." He replied.

"Where?"

"Back there, in the chart room Mate, right behind you."

I looked back in the chart room. No one was there. I stuck my head through the door and looked around, no one. But the pencil was back in the chart by itself again. I went in and put it in the drawer. I checked the radar, and then made a visual inspection of the two ships. They were getting close, the nearest was about three miles. (That's close considering it takes a mile to turn one of these tankers.) At 0150 the closest ship, at 2 ½ miles off, turned to starboard and crossed behind us. Shortly after that, the other ship's bearing started closing, indicating that she had sped up. As we passed under the stern of the second ship, I altered our course to 278 as indicated on the chart. 2 ½ miles was close. We usually didn't want anything closer than three miles, and with all that water out there, there was no reason to get any closer. But that guideline was the present captain's guideline; I've seen that vary from one to five miles.

With the danger over, I got a cup of coffee and went out on the starboard wing for a few minutes. As I looked back toward the wheelhouse while leaning on the windbreak, I saw Tex at the wheel, the lume of the steering gyro repeater illuminating his face. As I looked out to sea toward the two other ships that were steaming off to our right, that scene of Tex at the wheel stuck in my mind and gave me a very uneasy feeling, and I looked back to see what it was that bothered me. What I found was, from where I was standing, I couldn't see the helmsman. I had either imagined seeing him, or I had looked through the bulkhead of the wheelhouse because there was neither door nor window in the area between us. I walked over to the door, and looked in; the scene was just as I had seen it.

I walked over the gyro repeater on the wing and checked it; it read 288. But the course was 278. I went into the wheelhouse.

"Tex, what are you steering?"

"278 Mate, on the gyro."

I walked over behind him and checked over his shoulder; he was steering 278. I went back into the chart room and checked the course recorder; it was steady on 278. I went back out to the starboard wing and checked the gyro repeater; it read 288. I checked the port repeater, 288 also. I went up to the flying bridge, 288. I went into the gyro room; the master was at 278. Somehow the flying bridge and wing repeaters were all ten degrees off. I tried resetting the repeater on the port wing but couldn't get it to stay corrected. I made a mental note to tell the second mate as the navigation equipment was his responsibility.

I went into the chartroom to put a 0400 DR position on the chart, and there was the pencil again, on the chart. I knew I had put it in the drawer. I picked it up; John was still there. What was going on? John had never been there for more than a few minutes; this was going on two hours. I put the pencil back in the drawer and left the chartroom. I went into the pantry and got a cup of coffee. I was feeling unsettled and spent no more time in the wheelhouse that night. I didn't go in the chart room to fill out the log until the second came up to relieve me.

When the second mate looked at the chart, he immediately spotted the error. He had mislabeled the course on the chart. It should have been labeled 288. I was very uncomfortable standing in that chart room with Kevin while John was looking over my shoulder. I couldn't believe that Kevin didn't know about John. He was right there, standing next to us. How could Kevin work in that chart room as much as he did, and not know John was there?

The 278 course had put us on a heading toward the northern most rocks of Los Monjes, a group of small islands north of Punta Espada. There is a light on one of the southern islands but nothing on the northern ones. At 0400 we were still 23 miles off; but had I still been at the con at 0530, there might have been a problem. This was my first serious lesson on the necessity of checking the other officer's work when taking the con, and before taking any action; a lesson that I pounded into every third mate that sailed under me in later years.

With the heading properly adjusted to 296, the heading required to take us to safe water, John left and Kevin went up to the flying bridge to reset the repeater, but he found it, and the other two repeaters reading the correct heading - 296. He was probably wondering what I had been drinking that night.

The strange happenings that night were warnings from our supernatural guest. I thought he was telling me something about the traffic, because that's what I was most concerned about. But the warnings all seem to have pointed to a steering error, which, with a little more vigilance, I might have found and corrected. John didn't give up that night, he just kept pushing; I was the one that gave up. That night, I gave John a new name – Caretaker; and from that night on, I paid more attention to my navigation.

Chapter 23

Final Voyage

We rounded Los Monjes at a safe distance, and headed due west to get around the Peninsula de la Guajira. The return trip to Panama took only two days at our normal speed. I typed up the port log, completed my safety inspection and then went on to the crew list for Panama and the payroll. We arrived at 2300 on the 1st of January (I missed that holiday too), and started our transit the next morning. We anchored in Gatun Lake for six hours waiting for the northbound convoy to pass, so we could continue down through Gaillard Cut; continuing south at 1500 to Parita Bay. By midnight on the 3rd we made our approach to the *RESOLUTION* but had to scrub the berthing due to high winds and seas. Twelve hours later, the weather had settled down enough for us to go alongside, and we tied up with the BC surging against the *RESOLUTION* in high winds and a moderate sea. We had been working six hour shifts since the chief mate left in Panama two weeks earlier. Kevin had been moved up to chief mate with me being the second but still responsible for cargo operations. We started de-ballasting at 1400.

I was invited for drinks that evening by the officers of the *RESOLUTION* and made my way there at 2000 in my new good clothes, taking a chance that I'd ruin them climbing up the ladder. The ship was beautiful. Apparently, drinks are served every evening at 2000 on the *RESOLUTION* and evening dress is expected; that is dress whites. We had no uniforms, and even if we had, they wouldn't have been white for long. But the Brits tried to not make me feel like the bum I looked like, as I toured their operations center, officer's areas and the bridge deck. Drinks were served by waiters in a room that must have been some sort of an officer's lounge, though it looked too formal for me. They sure do lead a different kind of life. One should be prepared with proper training in British etiquette before attending one of these functions. English ship's officers have to be born into that station; they carry themselves with that knowledge, and have a certain expectation of being treated as members of nobility.

I might have been a peer with them but I didn't feel like it. American merchant officers are shown little respect by the companies they work for, as indicated by the conditions of their work place, and their rude treatment by company employees and managers. In America, by the 1970s it had become common to treat those of accomplishment with disdain; and those of little ambition or accomplishment seemed to think they cast the longest shadows, though they were merely standing in the shadows of others. Hard work had in fact become something to avoid.

I was back on deck for watch at midnight on the 4th to help complete the de-ballasting operations, and switch over to loading. We lost the pumps many times that morning with the ship surging as we were trying to strip out the tanks. Gauging that morning showed traces of water in most of the tanks due to our movement during the process. The new third mate came out at 0555, shortly after we started loading. By midnight, on the 5th we were loaded and ready to depart, again waiting for the weather to subside. Eighteen hours we lay alongside in weather too dangerous to work lines. We departed at 1900, and steamed up to Panama City, where we anchored for a few hours to wait a transit slot. We entered the canal at 0130 on the 6th. This was my 18th and last transit of the canal, much of which I saw from the stern.

We cleared the Gatun Locks at 1248 and took departure from Cristobal, heading north to Texas City in moderate seas with a twelve-foot swell on the starboard bow, and a twenty knot wind from ahead soaking the deck. We were rolling a bit, about three to five degrees, and there was some pitching; so the table cloths were soaked and I had that relaxing sound of the seashore background to try to sleep by. I'd been living in water world for two months by then and had abandoned hope of ever being on a dry deck in my room. As for the engineers, I had already replaced sixteen fire extinguishers and wondered if I had enough spares for the rest of the voyage.

For almost three weeks we had been working 18-20 hour days, without a chief mate, and I would have been exhausted if I hadn't been preoccupied with my impending release. My time was up and I would be going home. I had notified the captain about getting a replacement while we were in Parita Bay. He suggested that I stay on a while longer, like maybe another two months. (That's about the time he would be getting off.) I declined; six months was long enough.

We were moving about quite a bit, so I went out on deck and gathered the life rings before going on watch. Later, on the bridge, I took my last look at the wrecks on Quito Sueno on the afternoon of the 7th, with the seas growing. The wind was on the port bow at around thirty knots, with fifteen to twenty foot seas dead ahead. We were in Force 7 weather making about eleven knots being blown toward the banks. The BC was starting to pound and shudder as the seas occasionally broke over the bow. The deck was awash with the swells. I changed the course to 328 at 1412 to pass west of Misteriosa Bank, easing the ship a little, and bringing the seas back to the starboard bow. The sky was clear and cloudless, with the sun reflecting off thousands of whitecaps. This looked like just a big blow, nothing else. The weather reports showed high winds and seas, but no significant weather systems.

We held another Fire and Boat drill on the afternoon of the 8th. I got the port boat again and kept the crew longer to get procedures straightened out. I explained to them that when they got to the boat, they were supposed to start the process of getting the boat ready to launch. If I didn't make it to the boat, that didn't mean that they were supposed to go down with the ship. I told them that when I arrived, they should already be about their work. The only order I should have to give is "Lower the boat". I hoped that I had gotten the message across, because this was my last boat drill.

I had to fill out the ship's custom's papers that evening. We had had repairs in two foreign ports and there was a 50% duty on foreign repairs if the repairs were not absolutely necessary for the safe navigation of the ship. Ours were necessary so there was no problem other than documenting them properly.

The seas had picked up; dinner was challenging, or more to the point, difficult. We were rolling a good ten degrees with an occasional jolt as we slammed into a wave head on. I packed a night lunch before I left the mess hall. I didn't plan to make the trip before midnight.

When I took the con at midnight, we were in high to very high seas. We were in a bad spot, in the southern reaches of the Yucatan Channel where the current was three knots northerly with a fifty-knot north wind and thirty plus foot seas. A northerly current flows north, but a north wind comes from the north and is opposite a northerly current, which makes the seas steep. The bulwarks of our bow were about twenty-six feet above the sea, and the seas were somewhere between twenty-five and thirty feet high. When the ship went into a trough, the bow dipped down, and in our current condition, it was about six feet below the crest of the waves. We had a lot of water on deck, and even loaded, we were getting racking stress. I opened up the door to the chronometers and put my night lunch in there for safekeeping.

10.5 knots is all we were making. The caretaker stopped in for a few minutes to see how we were doing. I guess he was satisfied. The watch went by painstakingly slow. I ate my night lunch, and watched the radar. The sea clutter went out six miles, and the steering was swinging four degrees. I had Sundi put it on hand steering to see if he could do any better. After fifteen minutes, I had him change back. Conditions were the same when Kevin relieved me. The good news was that my room was practically empty. The rolling was washing most of the water over the threshold and into the passageway. Bonus – The chief engineer was really ticked off when he came up in the morning and found the passageway flooded. Other people's problems may be something to feel bad about, and even offer sympathy for but when they become your problem, they're something to fix. The third assistant engineer was looking over my room that morning to see if he could find the problem.

On the afternoon watch, we were in the south gulf, out of the current, and in well moderated seas. The swells were still twenty feet high but the period was longer, the pounding had ceased and the roll had diminished. The down side was that the water level in my room had resumed its earlier proportions; the third couldn't find the problem. After dinner, there was a knock on my door.

"It's open." I called out.

The door opened. "What the...!" The second engineer shouted out as he put his foot in three inches of water. "He said you had a little water. How long's it been like this?"

"Over two months now."

"You been slopping around in this for two months? This is a broken pipe someplace."

"I can't seem to get anyone to look at it."

"We gotta fix this. Where's it comin from?"

"The locker."

He stepped in, soaking his other shoe. "Hey, this is cold." He waded over to the locker, opened it and looked in. "There's nothing in there, I'm gonna have to go look at the piping." On the way out he stopped at the door. "Hey, what happened to your lock?"

"Three months ago."

"Gees Louise!" He went out and closed the door.

On the midnight watch, having cleared the Bank of Campeche, we were heading northwest toward Texas City in moderate seas, with a long slow roll. Traffic was starting to pick up as we approached the oil fields. At lunch the engineers had an interesting conversation. The chief and first were eating when the second came in.

"Hey Chief," he said as he sat down and took the menu. "I think we found your fresh water."

"Huh?"

"We found your fresh water, you know, you been complaining for two months that we been using too much fresh water. We found it, or rather, the third mate found it."

"Tom, how much water you got in your room?" the chief engineer asked me.

"Chief, I've been telling you for two months, my rooms flooded. It's four inches deep at the threshold, five at the outside. It's running over the threshold, into the passageway and down on the tween deck. Somebody's got to be able to fix this."

"Geeze, I thought you were exaggerating. I thought you had a puddle in there from a leaky valve or something."

"Hey, I've got to get up to the bridge. Can someone figure out how to shut that thing off?"

"Yeah, I'll get it fixed." the second answered. But it wasn't fixed that evening.

I was navigating through the oil rigs on the morning of the 11th, still in moderate seas. The morning went smoothly until Kevin came up at 0400. First he was upset because I had the steering auto pilot in rough seas. He said the autopilot couldn't handle it, so he had his ordinary put the steering on hand. Actually, it was doing fine as indicated on the course recorder, and as they say, "Contra factum, non est argumentum" (Against a fact, there is no argument – a little ditty by Thomas Aquinas). Then he started taking bearings on the wrong oil rigs, putting him two miles off position. There was nothing close, so I let him have his way. I knew he'd figure it out before the other third came up at 0800. By the time I went below, he had blown his top because his ordinary couldn't steer a good course in rough seas, so he had him put it back on autopilot. Kevin just was not a morning person.

I went below to my pond and gathered all of my clothes that were in bad shape from wear or stains and stacked them on my rack. I only kept my new good clothes and one set of work clothes. I gathered the rest and took them out to the passageway. After donning my socks and shoes, I took them all with me down to the main deck, and one by one dropped them over the side, watching each one as it was caught by the swirling water coming down the side of the ship. That would lighten my load a bit.

I got up early and had breakfast, so I could spend the morning packing the things I had left. What was I going to do with all that soap? The bottom drawer was full when I got on, and now a third of the top drawer was also filled. I put the soap from the top drawer in my duffle, and also took out ten bars from the bottom drawer. That way the new third mate would have space for the first month while he figured out where he would go from there.

I was on the bridge at noon as we were approaching the sea buoy. I pulled out the charts from earlier in the morning; it was just as I suspected. At 0400 the course jumped two miles to the right and ran that way until about 0540, when it jumped back to the center. I knew he'd figure it out. I put the charts back. Captain Daniels came up to the bridge at 1300 and called ARRIVAL at 1312. I had the other third mate called for docking at 1400, then the captain got on my case for not telling him that the lock on my door was broken, and that my room was flooded. He either forgot that he helped get the door open, or wanted to disavow all knowledge of it, for the record. I didn't know what the game was there, but I hadn't been silent about either of those things. I went back to the stern to work lines when the third came up to the bridge. We knocked off at 1700, secure and All Fast. Then I had to go to the captain's office to work the payroll. We finished that up at 2000.

The new third mate had arrived; it was a classmate of mine from the academy; who'd figure? It made it all the more difficult to give him the tour. I put my bags next to the 26 fire extinguishers waiting to go ashore to get recharged, and then took the new third up to the swamp. I told him that they were working on it and should have it fixed soon. That wasn't a lie, at least not an intentional lie. I really expected the engineers to get that problem fixed soon because they now knew that they were loosing fresh water because of it; but you'd have to check with the new third to see if that actually happened. I went over the paper work with him; that is the paper work he was supposed to do; not the chief mate's or the captain's. With everything taken care of, I stopped by the captain's office to say good-by. He was at his desk with some guy from the company discussing the ship's business. As I approached, I heard the company man say.

"I don't know who's been doing the cargo papers, but they're all fouled up."

The captain distracted him, and as he looked down, the captain waved me off with his right hand. He wanted me out of there before this guy found out who I was. Well, what goes around comes around. I kept the Panamanians off him, and he was keeping the company off me. I went below, picked up my gear, and I, and my 51 bars of soap, walked down that gangway for the last time.

Epilogue

Unbelievably, the *BALTIMORE CANON* huffed and puffed her way along for another twenty years, undoubtedly with a new owner that invested some money in her. I occasionally heard the name mentioned, which brought about some anxiety for a moment or two, until I remembered that for me, it was in the past. I remember the lack of visibility on the bridge with those three portholes, that eerie sound under the door to the tween deck that sounded like voices, the steam winches on deck that would hiss and bang as the steam was turned on and the condensed water purged through the valves, living in the swamp, and of course, the Caretaker. I was glad to get away from the BC for all of its problems, but I had just a little regret on leaving John behind. No one else seemed to be aware of him, and I didn't think I would ever come across him again (to my knowledge, I haven't). I still wonder if anyone else knew of him, who he was, or why he was there. I know that many who read this, will not believe that part of this story, and I guess that doesn't really matter; but I hope someone knows and can tell me more about him. He is the one figure in my career that still haunts my memory.

The overtime situation on the *BALTIMORE CANON* grew from 135 hours on my first month to well over 200 on each of the last few months. I was never compensated for the disputed overtime (about thirty hours) that I claimed for restriction to ship while anchored in a safe port in Panama, but I didn't request it to get the money. The purpose was to force the issue about launch service; and indeed we got that service from then on.

The operation we were involved in (the Parita Bay Trans-shipment Terminal) only lasted until 1982 when they completed a pipeline across Panama to expedite the service and reduce the cost of shipping oil east. The *BRITISH RENOWN* was hit by two missiles in the Persian gulf in 1984 causing light damage and both the *RENOWN* and *RESOLUTION* are no longer in service and have both been scrapped.

Marine transportation is a dangerous business and to demonstrate that more fully, I've included a short list of marine accidents that took place in our coastal waters during my tenure on the *Baltimore Canon*. This is not a comprehensive list; it only includes accidents investigated by the Marine Transportation Safety Board in our coastal waters. With the information in the addendum, you may, by extrapolation, get a better grasp on the magnitude of the inherent dangers of this occupation, worldwide.

In the six months that I rode the *BALTIMORE CANON*, I developed a few habits and instincts that have stayed with me, and particularly gave me trouble for the first few months that I was ashore. There were little things that probably made me look eccentric and some big things that probably made me out to be somewhat of a nut.

There was no barber on the ship, so I hadn't had a haircut in six months putting my hair down past my shoulders. I may have neglected to mention this in the previous chapters simply because hair grows slowly and one gets used to it. I would sometimes trim my hair to the extent that I needed to function as a ship's officer, including navigating with a sextant on the bridge wing in the wind. I would simply comb my hair forward and cut it so that it wouldn't get in my eyes when the wind was blowing. This gave it a Prince Valiant look, which nick name I was awarded by my family, when I arrived home. My mother didn't initially recognize me, and assuming that I was a friend of my brother's, asked if I would like to stay for dinner. I replied that I would indeed, and that I had in fact, once lived in the area. The voice and odd response were enough to open her eyes and ...well...

There was the phone problem. I had the habit of picking up the handset upside down, holding it like a microphone, and answering it with "Bridge" or "This is the *BALTIMORE CANON*". I was then usually, momentarily baffled by the lack of response of the caller, as there was no speaker in the phone body. More than once I asked those around me why these people called and then hung up without saying anything. I mostly worked that one out in a few days, but every once in a while I looked pretty stupid.

There was also the evening problem. If I was outside, or driving a car and the sun was getting low, I would extend my arm and measure the height of the sun above the horizon with my fingers. I knew I had five minutes per finger before I had to take an azimuth of the sun to check the accuracy of the gyro compass. Of course, I didn't need to check the compass, as there was none, which made explanations rather awkward, as most company had no idea what I was talking about.

I couldn't seem to get around the 12-4 watch schedule ashore. I was up until five in the morning most mornings, and slept until 11. I also had a hard time with the days of the week. On the ship, they're all the same. I frequently found myself going to the bank on Sunday to find it closed.

Then, there was the big dinner, the homecoming dinner, with the good china, fancy tablecloth, etc. I was the last one called because I was the guest of honor. Without thinking, I sat down, moved all my dinnerware to the side and proceeded to pour water from the water pitcher, all over my section of the table, thoroughly soaking the place, before moving everything back. I looked up and everyone was looking at me, with their mouths hanging open. One of my sisters asked what I was doing, and I replied. "We don't want the plates to ...move?" That was embarrassing. I looked down, and noticed my feet wrapped around the chair legs to keep it from sliding around.

Addendum

Marine Accidents from July- December

8/27/78 - Title: Collision of American Containership SS Sea-Land Venture and Danish Tanker M/T Nelly Maersk Inner Bar Channel, Galveston, Texas, August 27, 1978.**NTSB Report Number:** MAR-79-16, adopted on 9/27/1979**NTIS Report Number:** PB80-108657

About 0340 c.d.t., on August 27, 1978, the American containership SS SEA-LAND VENTURE collided with the Danish tanker M/T NELLY MAERSK when the SEA-LAND VENTURE attempted to overtake the NELLY MAERSK in the Galveston-Houston Ship Channel. There were no injuries or deaths. Damage to the vessels was estimated at $1.4 million. The National Transportation Safety Board determines that the probable cause of the accident was the inaccurate evaluation of the closing rate and late initiation of the rudder order by the pilot of the SEA-LAND VENTURE while attempting to overtake the NELLY MAERSK at a bend in a narrow channel where the risk of collision was much greater than in a straight portion of the channel.

9/23/78 - Title: Fishing Vessel M/V Lobsta-1 Capsizing and Sinking in the Atlantic Ocean point Judith, Rhode Island, September 23, 1978**NTSB Report Number:** MAR-80-06, adopted on 4/16/1980**NTIS Report Number:** PB80-1830

About 0100 E.D.T., on September 23, 1978, the fishing vessel MV LOBSTA-I capsized in the Atlantic Ocean about 47 nmi south-southeast of Point Judith, Rhode Island, while en route to its lobster fishing area. The capsized vessel was sighted about 12 hours after the accident by a tankship. Subsequently, a Coast Guard helicopter sighted the capsized vessel but it sank before the Coast Guard cutter could reach it. The Coast Guard conducted an extensive search in the area but found no survivors. The LOBSTA-I was later located resting upright on the bottom at a 234-ft water depth, and photographs, showing damage to the vessel's hull plating were taken by a shipboard controlled, underwater vehicle. All five crewmen are missing and presumed dead. The Safety Board considered many factors during the investigation, including vessel stability, operating practices, weather forecasting, and the possibility of collision. The National Transportation Safety Board is unable to determine the probable cause of the capsizing of the LOBSTA-I. Vessel damage indicates a collision with another vessel as a possible cause of the capsizing; however, the evidence is not sufficient to establish that such a collision occurred. Another possible, but less likely, cause is the loss of stability due to internal flooding. The lack of distress notification may have contributed to the loss of life.

10/3/78 - Title: Collision of the S/T Texaco Iowa and the M/T Burmah Spar on the Mississippi River Pilottown, Louisiana, October 3, 1978.**NTSB Report Number:** MAR-80-03, adopted on 2/14/1980**NTIS Report Number:** PB80-158249

At 0420, on October 3, 1978, the ST TEXACO IOWA collided with the MT BURMAH SPAR while both tank vessels were inbound and maneuvering in the pilot exchange area off Pilottown, Louisiana. The total damage to the vessels was estimated at $680,000. No persons were injured in this accident. The National Transportation Safety Board determines that the probable cause of this accident was the failure of the bar pilot and the master to navigate the TEXACO IOWA at a safe distance from the BURMAH SPAR while maneuvering to change pilots. Contributing to the accident was the TEXACO IOWA bar pilot's misjudgment of the vessels' relative speeds and his failure to observe the Inland Rules of the Road, the delayed reaction of the master of the TEXACO IOWA in directing evasive maneuvers, and the failure of the pilots to establish bridge-to-bridge radiotelephone communications before the collision.

10/20/78 - Title: Collision of Argentine Freighter M/V Santa Cruz II and U.S. Coast Guard Cutter Cuyahoga in Chesapeake Bay, mouth of

Potomac River, MD Oct. 20, 1978**NTSB Report Number:** MAR-79-03, adopted on 2/26/1979**NTIS Report Number:** PB-293461/AS

At 2107 E.D.T. on October 20, 1978, the Argentine freighter MV SANTA CRUZ II and the U.S. Coast Guard cutter CUYAHOGA collided in Chesapeake Bay at the mouth of the Potomac River, Maryland. As a result of the collision, the CUYAHOGA sank. Eleven Coast Guardsmen were killed; 18 Coast Guardsmen were rescued by the SANTA CRUZ II which experienced minor damage. The National Transportation Safety Board determines that the probable cause of this accident was the left turn executed by the CUYAHOGA, while in proximity to the SANTA CRUZ II, contrary to the Rules of the Road as the vessels were meeting head and head; the failure of the Commanding Officer of the CUYAHOGA to determine the relative motion, course, speed, or closest point of approach of the SANTA CRUZ II; and, the failure of the CUYAHOGA to initiate bridge-to-bridge communications by radiotelephone to exchange navigational information. Contributing to the loss of life was the lack of emergency lighting aboard the CUYAHOGA.

10/25/78 - Title: R/V Don J Miller II Collision with the F/V Welcome Admirality Inlet Puget Sound, Washington, October 25, 1978.**NTSB Report Number:** MAR-79-14, adopted on 9/25/1979**NTIS Report Number:** PB-301202/AS

On the evening of October 25, 1978, the research vessel R/V DON J. MILLER II, inbound to Seattle, Washington, collided with the fishing vessel F/V WELCOME in Admiralty Inlet. Shortly thereafter, the WELCOME sank. There were no deaths or serious injuries. Damage to the MILLER was negligible; the WELCOME was a total loss estimated at $300,000. The National Transportation Safety Board determines that the probable cause of this accident was the MILLER's master leaving the control of his vessel unattended while the MILLER was still the burdened vessel in an overtaking situation. Contributing to the accident were the failure of the WELCOME to ascertain the whereabouts of the MILLER before changing course, and the failure of both the MILLER and the WELCOME to maintain proper lookouts.

11/9/78 - Title: Collision of Greek Bulk Carrier M/V Irene S. Lemos and Panamanian Bulk Carrier M/V Maritime Justice, near New Orleans, Louisiana, Nov. 9, 1978.**NTSB Report Number:** MAR-80-04, adopted on 2/14/1980**NTIS Report Number:** PB80-163355

At 0640 C.S.T., on November 9, 1978, the Greek bulk carrier MV IRENE S. LEMOS and the Panamanian bulk carrier MV MARITIME JUSTICE collided in the Lower Mississippi River at mile 78.3 AHP, about 15 statute miles below New Orleans, Louisiana. Because of dense fog, the visibility at the time of the collision was less than 400 feet. The vessels struck nearly head-on, damaging the bows of both vessels. There were no deaths or injuries. Cost of repairs to the two vessels was estimated at $4 million. About 1,800 barrels of fuel oil were discharged into the Mississippi River and resulted in local health officials securing the municipal water intake 1/2 mile downriver. The National Transportation Safety Board determines that the probable causes of the accident were the poor judgment of the pilots of the MARITIME JUSTICE and the IRENE S. LEMOS when they agreed to meet and pass, in near zero visibility conditions, at English Turn Bend, where the risk of collision was much greater than in a straight portion of the river, and the failure of the vessels to move to the extreme right of the channel. Contributing to the accident was the failure of the mate on the MARITIME JUSTICE and the master of the IRENE S. LEMOS to exercise their responsibility to assure that the vessels were navigated safely, rather than indiscriminately relying on the pilots of the vessels.

12/29/78 - Title: Collision of the M/V World Nobility and the S/S Pennsylvania Getty at the Mouth of the Chesapeake Bay, near Norfolk, Virginia, December 29, 1978.**NTSB Report Number:** MAR-79-07, adopted on 5/31/1979**NTIS Report Number:** PB-296888/AS

About 1819 E.S.T., on December 29, 1978, the outbound Liberian bulk carrier MV WORLD NOBILITY and the inbound Liberian ore/bulk/oil (OBO) carrier SS PENNSYLVANIA GETTY collided at the mouth of the Chesapeake Bay about 15 nautical miles east of Norfolk, Virginia. The bow of the PENNSYLVANIA GETTY penetrated the No.1 cargo hold on the forward port side of the WORLD NOBILITY. There were no deaths or injuries resulting from the accident. Damage to the vessels was estimated at about $3 million. The National Transportation Safety Board determines that the probable causes of this accident were the failure of the masters of the WORLD NOBILITY and PENNSYLVANIA GETTY to maneuver their vessels safely because of inattention, and their failure to comply with the International Regulations for Preventing Collisions at Sea. Contributing to the accident was the location of the Chesapeake Bay pilotage area, necessitating both vessels to transit an area subject to heavy converging traffic without the assistance of pilots.

12/78 - Title: Sinking of the M/V Holoholo in the Pacifc Ocean, near the Hawaiian Island, December 1978.**NTSB Report Number:** MAR-80-15, adopted on 9/19/1980**NTIS Report Number:** PB82-171646

About 1437, on December 9, 1978, the MV HOLOHOLO departed Honolulu Harbor, Island of Oahu, on the second of six planned 6-day voyages involving an Ocean Thermal Energy Conversion research project that the University of Hawaii had contracted to perform over a 1-year period at a site centered about 17 nmi west of Kawaihae, Island of Hawaii. The 10 persons on board were the owner, a licensed master of research vessels, a hydraulic mechanic, and 7 scientists associated with the research to be conducted. The voyage intinerary included plans to rendezvous with two scientists who were to board the vessel in Kawaihae Harbor at daybreak on December 11, 1978, but the HOLOHOLO did not arrive as planned. Despite an extensive air-sea search by the Coast Guard, the Navy, the Air Force, the University, and others, the HOLOHOLO was not found. The National Transportation Safety Board determines that the probable cause of this accident was the operation of the MV HOLOHOLO in an unseaworthy condition as directed by the owner and accepted by the Research Corporation of the University of Hawaii. Contributing to the vessel's unseaworthiness were a 2-ft by 4-ft opening in the after main deck and a large opening in the aftermost deckhouse bulkhead that would allow rapid internal flooding, unsealed below-deck bulkhead penetrations that would allow progressive flooding, inadequate freeing ports that would allow shipped water to be trapped on deck, and the insufficient number of qualified operating personnel to provide a 24-hour navigation watch. The lack of a distress signal or radio message might have contributed to the loss of life.

From the National Transportation Library, NTL Integrated Search, National Transportation Safety Board, TRIS Online, http://ntlsearch.bts.gov/tris/index.do

Glossary

Abeam - Directly off the side of the ship or ninety degrees from both the bow and stern.

AB - Able Body Seaman

Able Body Seaman - An experienced seaman capable of steering, operating the ships mechanical deck equipment and carrying a life boatman's certificate.

Arrival – The time the ship finishes a voyage as it passes the sea buoy on its way into the destination port.

Azimuth - A bearing by degree of an object in relation to true north.

Azimuth Circle - A device placed over the compass repeater by which azimuths can be taken. This device is usually kept in a protective case when not in use.

Ballast - Additional weight added to a ship to make it more stable. Permanent ballast can be iron, concrete, stone or other heavy material that will not shift around. Tank ships use sea water loaded into permanent ballast tanks or sometimes cargo tanks, which can be discharged easily when preparing to load cargo.

Barrel - 40 gallons, the measure used in the transportation of oil.

Beam - The width of a ship at its maximum.

Berth – A place for a ship to secure itself to work cargo.

Binnacle - The tabernacle which houses the ships magnetic compass.

Boatswain – The Bo's'n, or Bos'n, a day worker, the head of the deck crew. He takes orders from the Chief Mate and directs the deck crew to carry them out.

Bos'n – Boatswain.

Bow line – Mooring line attached to the dock forward of the bow.

Breast line – Mooring line attached to the dock straight out from the bow and stern.

Bridge – The space from which the ship is commanded.

Broad on the Beam – An object that is bearing ninety degrees from the ships head or straight off the side of the ship.

Bulkhead – A wall.

Bunkers – Bunker C, a fuel oil used in steam ships. This is also known as Number 6 Fuel Oil. It is a heavy tarry residue from the oil refining process that needs to be heated up to 140 degrees F to flow, and 600 degrees F to burn.

Captain – The commander of the ship.

Cavitate – Voids in a fluid caused by the vacuum created when an impeller or propeller is moving too fast for the amount of fluid available.

Celestial – Having to do with the sky and the stars.

Chief Engineer – In charge of the Ship's engine space and engine crew. A day worker, not a watch stander, on call 24 hours a day.

Chief Mate – In charge of the deck department, deck crew, ship's operations and cargo operations. A day worker, not a watch stander, on call 24 hours a day.

Chief Officer – The Chief Mate.

Coaming – A vertical structure to prevent low water from flowing between rooms or into hatches.

Con – Control. Figure of speech. Taking or releasing control of the ship by the captain at his prerogative from or to the watch officer.

Dead Reckoning – A position charted only taking into considering the ship's heading and speed by propeller revolutions.

Demurrage – The cost of a ship alongside a dock without working cargo.

Departure – The point that the ship starts a voyage as it passes the sea buoy of the port it is leaving.

Dog Watch – In the navy the dog watches are from 1600 to 1800 and 1800 to 2000. In the merchant marine it's the time the 4-8 officer is relieved on the bridge so he can go below for dinner, usually about 1655 to 1720.

DR – Dead Reckoning

Engine Order Telegraph - The equipment used to relay engine orders from the bridge to the engine room.

EOT – Engine Order Telegraph.

EP – Estimated Position

Estimated Position – A position charted taking into consideration the ship's heading, speed and set and drift of the current as experienced locally.

ETA – Estimated Time of Arrival

Faking – A method of laying out the mooring lines on deck so they can run free without tangling.

Fantail – The deck area furthest aft.

First Mate – The Chief Mate.

First Officer - The Chief Mate.

First Assistant Engineer – The senior engineering watch standing officer.

Flotsam – Garbage or wreckage floating in the water.

Fo'c'sle – An abbreviation for forecastle.

Fo'c's'le – Another abbreviation for forecastle.

Forecastle – A raised deck at the bow providing protected storage space for equipment.

Hog – A condition caused by improper distribution of cargo where the bow and stern are loaded heavier than the mid-section.

Hook – Slang for the anchor.

Jacob's Ladder – A rope ladder with wooden rungs used to board the ship from a small boat.

Jamb (Valve) – Opening a valve too far so it sticks.

Jetsam – Garbage or wreckage that you've thrown into the water.

Knot – One nautical mile per hour.

Latitude – Earth measurement starting at 0 degrees at the equator and increasing to 90 degrees at the poles.

Ladder – A stairway.

League – Measure of distance. Approximately three miles for the English, the distance a man can walk in one hour for Latin America.

Longitude – Earth measurement starting at 0 degrees on the Greenwich meridian and increasing to 180 degrees east or west at the international dateline.

Longitudinal – A ship's framing member running the length of the ship connecting to the ship's transverse framing. The ship's skin is attached to it.

Long Ton – 2240 pounds

LORAN A – Electronic long range navigation system using radio wave time delay, shut down in the early 1980s.

LORAN C – Electronic long range navigation system using radio wave time delay, still in use.

Manifold – Cargo pipe configuration where shore side connections are made.

Marlinspike Seamanship – Work involving the use of natural, synthetic, and wire rope in knots and splicing.

Master – The captain.

Mid-ships – Mid-way between the bow and stern. Also a steering command to place the rudder at 0 degrees.

Morse Code – A code of signals devised by Samuel Morse made of a series of dots and dashes to communicate by radio, signal light or flag.

Nautical Mile – the distance of one minute of latitude at the equator or about 6080 feet.

North Star – Polaris, a star usually within one degree of north from anywhere on earth.

Ordinary Seaman – An apprentice seaman studying and working toward becoming an Able Body Seaman.

OS – Ordinary Seaman, the lowest man on the deck crew.

Overhead – The ceiling on a ship.

Parted – Snapped, or broke apart.

Passageway – A hallway on a ship.

Polaris – the North Star, a star usually bearing within one degree of north from anywhere in the northern hemisphere.

Port – Left, also a seaport, a place where ships can dock or anchor.

Post – To set someone at a task. Also to display something.

Rack – in a cabin the rack is the cot or bed.

Racking – caused by sheer stresses which in turn are caused by the unequal pressure on the hull created by the forward thrust of the engines against the resistance of the ocean, and is magnified in heavy seas as the bow plows into high waves.

RADAR – Radio Detecting And Ranging, a device emitting radio waves and indicating reflections on a scope. Ship's usually had two RADAR units, a 10 cm for long distance and 3 cm for shorter range..

Range – Two lights used to steer on, separated by a horizontal distance, and located on the shore along an extended line of a channel, the further light being higher than the nearer, so that when the lights are both visible, one over the other, the navigator can be sure the ship is in the channel. Also means –distance- as in radar range.

RPMs – Revolutions per minute of the shaft and propeller.

Sag - A condition caused by improper distribution of cargo where the bow and stern are loaded lighter than the mid-section.

Scuttlebutt – A drinking fountain, also rumors, or news.

Sea Chest – Where the ballast line goes through the ship's hull.

Sea Chest Valves – The ballast line valves at the ship's hull.

Sea Clutter – Back scatter on the radar unit from reflections off waves, the higher the waves, the more scatter. Obstructs the radar view for miles in heavy seas.

Second Assistant Engineer – Experienced watch standing engineer.

Second Mate – Experienced watch standing bridge officer, also the ship's navigator.

Second Officer – The Second Mate.

Shanghaied – Taken against one's will or without one's knowledge to serve aboard a ship.

Shore time – The time a sailor spends ashore while not scheduled for work or on vacation.

Short Ton – 2000 pounds, not used in shipping.

"Slipped his cable" – Died.

Slop Chest – Slang for Ship's Store.

SOHIO – Standard Oil of Ohio, Rockefeller's company.

Sound Powered Phone – System using un-powered crystals to transport voice over copper.

Spring line – A mooring line attached to the dock forward of the stern or aft of the bow.

Starboard - Right

Steep to – A land mass with a coast of steep hills of cliffs. They give off a good radar reflection.

Stern line – A mooring line run out from the stern attached to the dock back from the stern.

Sun Line – A navigational line of position using the suns angular altitude from the horizon and an assumed position on the globe for a bearing to determine with high accuracy a single line of position. More than one is necessary to plot a fix, or the ship's actual position.

Taffrail – The railing around the stern.

Terrestrial – Having to do with land or land based systems.

Third Assistant Engineer – The lowest watch standing engineering officer.

Third Mate – The lowest watch standing deck officer, also the safety officer.

Third Officer – The Third Mate.

Thwart – The bench seat in a small boat that extends to both sides.

Transverse Beam - A ship's framing member running the width of the ship. The ship's longitudinals are attached to it.

Tween – Short for between. A tween deck is between other decks and may not run the entire length of the ship.

Ullage – The measurement from the cargo oil level in the cargo tank to the ullage hole in the tank top.

Valve – A device for controlling flow.

Valve jamb – Caused by opening a valve too far. A valve doesn't jamb closed because it's designed to close tight but it can jamb open.

VHF Radio – Very high frequency radio used for ship to ship and ship to shore communications.

Voice Tube – Copper tubes between critical spaces for communications when all else fails. There is a mechanical whistle plate in the tube so the caller can blow through the tube and sound the whistle at the other end. A small lever opens the plate so communications can be unobstructed.

Watch – A work shift of two, four-hour periods starting twelve hours apart. 00-04 and 12-16. 04-08 and 16-20. 08-12 and 20-24